Of Whales and
Women

by FRANK B. GILBRETH, JR., *and*
ERNESTINE GILBRETH CAREY

> *Cheaper by the Dozen*
> *Belles on Their Toes*

---

by FRANK B. GILBRETH, JR.

> *Held's Angels*
> *I'm a Lucky Guy*
> *Innside Nantucket*
> *Of Whales and Women*

Of Whales and Women

Women

One Man's View of Nantucket History

FRANK B. GILBRETH, Jr.

Illustrated by DONALD McKAY

THOMAS Y. CROWELL COMPANY, NEW YORK

FOREWORD

I would have finished this book several years ago, if I hadn't got all bogged down in the research. The fascinating old logs of the whaling captains kept me away from my typewriter—which some reviewers may consider a wholesome blessing—even after I had all the material I needed. And of course there was the matter of confirming my knowledge that Nantucket, Massachusetts, is a wonderful summer resort: Research along that line, which included lying half asleep on the beach, consumed weeks on end and extended over intervals of a number of years.

My paternal grandmother, who was a Maine Bunker and was married before the Civil War, visited Nantucket in the 1860s, when it was still a whaling town. My father started spending the summers there in the 1870s, when it was just becoming a fashionable resort. I first went there in the summer of 1918, and have returned annually except for three years during World War II, when I was in the Navy and had the privilege of visiting some of the South Sea Islands which were discovered by Nantucket whalemen some 130 years before.

I suppose I had better say unpretentiously, before some unkind crank says it for me, that this book purports to be no more than a "popular history" of Nantucket, combined with some of my own experiences there as a member of a large family. I've attempted to catch the flavor and spirit of old Nantucket, rather than to document every fact of history.

Just the same, I have gone to the source wherever I could, and the history herein is sound.

Aside from the old logs and the books and manuscripts of "recollections," I have relied for anecdotes principally on *Nantucket, the Far Away Island,* by William Oliver Stevens; *Yankee Whalers in the South Seas,* by A.B.C. Whipple; *An Island Patchwork,* by Eleanor Early; and *Nantucket Odyssey,* by Dr. Emil F. Guba. Mr. Stevens' book was the principal source for the stories of the Newbegin girls and Keziah Coffin.

For the chapter on Maria Mitchell, I leaned heavily on *Sweeper in the Sky,* by Helen Wright. And for the material on R. H. Macy, I drew from the *History of Macy's of New York,* by Professor Ralph M. Hower, and from *The Great Merchants,* by Tom Mahoney.

Several books about specialized phases of Nantucket, by the Rev. Dr. William E. Gardner, were helpful. So were two booklets entitled *Nantucket Argument Settlers,* edited by Harry B. Turner, and *Rambling Through the*

Streets and Lanes of Nantucket, by Edouard A. Stackpole.

The publishers of those books, and a list of other books on which I relied, are in the bibliography at the back.

It is customary in this sort of foreword also to mention the names of people who were helpful and offered encouragement. Instead, I am tempted to list those who diverted me from my chores at Nantucket by inviting me to go swimming, sailing, fishing, picnicking, bridge-playing, drinking and lobster-eating—temptations which I find difficult to resist at any location, and impossible to resist with pleasant company at Nantucket. High on this list I reluctantly must place my wife and all five of my brothers.

CONTENTS

Of Whales and
Women

1. A MATTER OF TASTE

"Morning, sir," said Jotham Marden, touching his fore-lock respectfully and being careful to keep a straight face. "I request thy permission to grease the lead."

The captain, a bearded and ancient Nantucket Quaker, looked past Marden and saw the assembled crew, grinning self-consciously. The Old Man had been asleep in his cabin when Marden knocked at the door. He was wide awake now, but he yawned and rolled over as if still only semi-conscious. "Permission granted," he sighed, closing his eyes again.

The captain had sailed so far and wide in his fifty-year career as a whaling master that his crew swore he could tell his location simply by tasting the bottom. They said that whenever his square-rigger was blown off course, he'd grease a sounding lead, toss it over the side, pull it

1

up, and taste the sand embedded in the grease. Then he'd plot his position.

The captain, a stern man but not without a sense of humor, did nothing to refute this extravagant claim.

His ship was always happy, as contrasted with taut, and it was deemed safe occasionally to play a trick on the Old Man. So when Jotham Marden, a skeptical new hand, had decided actually to test the captain's bottom-tasting ability, the rest of the crew had crowded aft to see whether their skipper would pass the exam.

Having obtained permission to grease the lead, Marden closed the door softly on the "sleeping" old timer. Immediately, the captain leaped spryly out of bed, tiptoed over to a porthole, and watched Marden and the crew emerge on deck. Marden carefully larded the lead. Then, while the crew doubled up in silent mirth, the skeptic dropped the lead into a box of soil on the deck—good soil which the captain had brought from Nantucket to keep fresh his favorite vegetable, parsnips.

Tiptoeing slyly back to his bunk, the captain was snoring loudly enough to jibe the spanker, when Marden knocked on his door again. Marden had to beat a regular tattoo before the snoring stopped and he was told sleepily to enter.

The captain managed to open one eye. "Yes?" he grunted.

"The lead, sir," said Marden.

"*What* lead?" yawned the Old Man, with apparent irritation.

"The greased lead, sir, that I dropped over the side," said Marden, and the skipper thought he detected a patronizing note in the seaman's voice. "Thee said thee would taste it and tell us where we are."

"Oh, *that* lead," the captain remembered, but still very sleepily. "I said thee could grease it. I said nothing about tasting it."

Marden glanced triumphantly over his shoulder at the crew standing outside the door.

"Thee doesn't wish to taste it, sir?" he gloated.

"What kind of whittling is this?" complained the captain, purposely employing the querulous tones of senility. "Can't a captain even get a nap aboard his own vessel? All right, man, give me the lead—anything to get rid of thee!"

Marden held out the lead. The captain, without rising, took it, yawned again, and extended a red little tongue through the white muff of his beard. Absently, he touched the lead to his tongue. Then, suddenly coming wide awake with incredulous disbelief, he quickly licked the lead again for confirmation.

In an instant, he was out of bed and thrusting his feet into his boots.

"Call all hands," he roared. "All hands on deck! Nantucket's sunk and we're right smack-dab over old Marm Hackett's vegetable garden!"

There hasn't been a whaleship out of Nantucket now for more than eighty years. And the descendants of the brave but prim Quaker captains, who were so proper they made their wives wear bonnets to bed, now earn a living by catering to bare-headed and bare-legged "trippers" in Bermuda shorts.

But in some ways, the cobblestoned, silver-sided Massa-

chusetts island thirty miles off Cape Cod hasn't changed at
all since the days when Nantucket was the whaling capital
of the world. Every breath of air there is still dusted pure
by the ocean. The Old Grist Mill, whose four outstretched
arms once were a secret signal telling returning whaleships whether the coast was clear of British frigates, is still
there. So are the houses in Orange Street, where 126
whaling captains lived in a row.

No town of comparable size in America has had as
much influence on the history of the world as Nantucket.

Nantucket whalemen were the first to understand and
map the Gulf Stream, and their findings revolutionized
the traffic patterns between the Old World and the New.
They were among the first to explore both the Arctic and
the Antarctic, and their discoveries are part of the basis
of American claims to Polar lands.

Although others had preceded them, they were the first
to beat a path around Cape Horn, and to chart the Pacific.
The "ile" and whalebone they brought back from the
Pacific lit the lamps and laced the ladies, wherever there
was civilization.

Nantucketers were the first link between the West and
Australia, New Zealand, China, and Hawaii. They were
worshiped as gods on some Pacific islands. They consorted
with the light-skinned, naked beauties of Polynesia and
they ate with and were eaten by the coal-black, fierce
Melanesians.

A Nantucketer brought to Boston the first news of the
repeal of the despised Stamp Act. Three Nantucket ships
sailed into Boston harbor with the tea for the famous Tea

Party. Another Nantucket ship was the first to hoist the Stars and Stripes in a British port.

A Nantucketer found the hiding place of the men who had staged the mutiny on the *Bounty*. Another mutiny, infinitely more gory, occurred on the Nantucket whaleship *Globe*.

The Nantucket story is recorded in scribbled sea chanties and hundreds of carefully written log books, now safely locked in the Nantucket Whaling Museum and the Atheneum library. The story is in the stately Main Street Mansions, built with sperm oil money and "greasy luck." It is in the snug gray lean-tos (on Cape Cod they are called salt-boxes), fashioned by ship's carpenters who thought that a house should be as honest and as functional as a full-rigged ship.

It is in the shingled, weather-beaten home where a doddering white cannibal once hid bits of food under the eaves of his roof.

It is in the thousand-and-one pieces of whale-tooth "scrimshaw"—crochet needles, walking sticks, delicate little wheels to crimp pie crust, toy parasols, ships' models —which adorn the keepin' rooms and bornin' rooms of the marvelous old houses; scrimshaw carved and holy-stoned smooth in foul-smelling forecastles and on torrid, tar-oozing decks, with the incredible patience of a generation which prized workmanship and wasn't in a hurry.

Nantucketers themselves haven't changed too much, either. True enough, they no longer catch whales. Instead, they now rent rooms and catboats to summer visitors, pump gasoline in filling stations, serve "ice cream and tonic" in drug stores, cook quahaug chowder and wash dishes in restaurants. But they still are independent, suspicious of authority, set in their ways, individualistic, and certain that the sun rises and sets on their island.

"Three souls and two New Bedforders were lost when the ship went down," is how one of the old Nantucket newspapers once reported a marine tragedy. And those who live on the back of the "Little Gray Lady of the Sea" still think of their own people in that light. On those rare occasions when the harbor freezes up solidly and Nantucket is out of communication with the rest of the world, the islanders report solemnly that the rest of the world is out of communication with Nantucket.

Nantucketers still have a sense of humor, however, and it doesn't seem to have changed much through the years. For instance, an old citizen named Cap'n Billy Baxter, who used to drive summer visitors over the moors in his surrey, sometimes employed the same sand-tasting joke as the aged, parsnip-loving whaling skipper. When a fog came up, Cap'n Billy would pretend he was lost, stop his horse, push his whip handle into the sand, and taste it experimentally.

"I calc'late we're 'bout three-quarters of a mile from Surfside," he'd inform his passengers. "Giddap, Lovey."

Billy Baxter was considerably before my time, but I often heard about him from my father. Baxter lived in the small settlement of Siasconset. Eight miles across the moors from Nantucket, 'Sconset had no Post Office until Cap'n Billy decided to open one. Without bothering to consult officials in Washington or Nantucket, he painted "POST OFFICE" in big letters on the side of his house, and appointed himself postmaster. From then on, he charged a penny apiece to take letters to Nantucket for mailing, or to bring letters from there.

Actually, he was performing a needed service. But when the word reached Washington that 'Sconset had a self-appointed postmaster, a postal inspector was dispatched to the scene of the crime.

Cap'n Billy got wind of this, possibly through some friend in the Nantucket Post Office. At any rate, when the inspector arrived at Nantucket by steamer, he was met at the wharf by an old character who was shouting, "Carriage for 'Sconset, carriage for 'Sconset."

"How much do you charge to drive to 'Sconset?" asked the inspector.

"Two dollars there and two dollars back," said Baxter. "Git in."

The inspector got in, and they started on a long drive through Nantucket town and across the moors.

"You don't happen to know a 'Sconset man named William Baxter, do you?" asked the inspector.

"Everyone knows William," nodded Cap'n Billy.

"What kind of a man would he be?"

"Odd as huckleberry chowder," conceded Baxter, all too truthfully. "But honest as the day is long, and both loved and highly respected by his many friends and neighbors."

"I understand he's opened a Post Office at 'Sconset—there's a big sign on his house that says so. And he calls himself the postmaster."

"Dew tell," Cap'n Billy remarked noncommittally.

"You never heard of his Post Office?"

"You'll have to see for yourself," said Baxter.

Meanwhile, he was steering the surrey over the roughest roads and ruts on the moors, working around in a circle aimed not at 'Sconset, but at the much smaller community of Polpis.

The circuitous trip to Polpis took four spine-jolting hours. And when Cap'n Billy finally stopped his surrey there, the exhausted inspector could see at a glance that there were only three or four houses, and certainly no Post Office.

"They sent me all the way from Washington on a wild-goose chase," complained the inspector. "When's the next steamer back to the mainland?"

"In an hour, and we kin still make it if we hurry," said Cap'n Billy, who saw no reason to take a roundabout way back. "Giddap, Lovey."

2. GOOD INDIANS, AND DEAD

Toward the end of World War I, my father bought two surplus lighthouses and the lightkeeper's toolshed on Nantucket, as summer headquarters for our family. The toolshed was expanded into a cottage, with a boys' dormitory, a girls' dormitory, kitchen, bath, dining room, bedroom for Dad and Mother and combination porch and living room.

There were eight children in the family at that time. Although the number subsequently increased to a dozen, the volume of noise had already leveled off on a plateau so high that Dad often preferred to sleep in one of the lighthouses, where he had a cot. The other lighthouse, smaller than Dad's, was furnished as a guest house.

The reason there were two lighthouses so close together was that they had served as "bug lights." Dad's lighthouse

was three stories tall and the guest room lighthouse two
stories. In the old days, when a mariner saw the tall light
directly over the short light, he knew he was lined up
correctly to enter the harbor's channel. The bug lights
originally burned whale oil, and they were built in 1838.

My father thought it part of the job of parenthood to
help educate his children. He was a supremely self-confi-
dent man, and there was no doubt in his mind that he
performed this job superbly—infinitely better than the
teachers who taught us during nine months of the year in
schools at Montclair, New Jersey. Just the same, he recognized the value of having certain specialists join his unofficial summer faculty, as visiting professors.

So he carefully selected his house guests at Nantucket
—or at any rate his lighthouse guests—with the premeditated purpose of adding to our education.

One week, the guest might be an astronomer such as
Dr. Harlow Shapley of Harvard. The next week a botanist.
The next an ornithologist. Captain Billy Baxter almost cer-
tainly would have called some of Dad's friends (but not
Dr. Shapley) "as odd as huckleberry chowder."

One friend, a retired museum curator or assistant curator, was an outstanding authority on Indian lore. And
he's the man who first got me interested in looking up the
history of Nantucket Indians.

He came originally from Maine, as did my father, and
he had become so engrossed in his subject that he not
only often acted and thought like an Indian, but almost
always smelled like one. My brothers and sisters and I
called him, for obvious reasons and of course behind his
back, Chief Nosoap.

He was a short, thin, spry, angry-looking man in his seventies, with plenty of long and heavy white hair, worn in belligerent General Custer fashion as if offering a dare to would-be scalpers. He had a pinched face and a generous nose, and he wore thick-lens, *pince-nez* glasses which magnified his watery blue eyes so that they seemed to take up the whole top of his head. Despite these heavy glasses, there wasn't very much that he missed.

When he spoke, it was largely in grunted monosyllables. He liked his meat almost raw, and I'm sure that some of his deplorable table manners must have been affectations —because certainly he knew better.

Also, he carried a filthy clay pipe—the kind that old Irishmen named Pat and Mike always used to carry in the cartoons—and often would stop along the roadside and fill it scientifically with some particular species of dried herb or leaves. Then he'd light the pipe with a match struck across the seat of his khaki knickers—although you could tell that if he had the time he would prefer to rub two sticks together, or at least to pull a glowing coal out of a campfire's embers. After a few tentative puffs, he'd nod as if he were satisfied, and then inhale contentedly. I found out later that he was looking for a weed named *poke,* which the Indians once used instead of tobacco. But I think he finally satisfied himself that *poke* no longer grew on Nantucket.

We all became very fond of Chief Nosoap, particularly after we discovered that his angry look did not reflect his personality, and that there was hardly any chance at all he would tomahawk us. We usually tried to keep him to leeward, though. And during the week he stayed with us,

Mother arranged it so that almost every meal except breakfast was a "squantum," as the Chief said the early Nantucketers called beach picnics.

I think it was about 1919 that the Chief visited us—
and that would have made me eight years old at the time.
My clearest memory of him is on an afternoon I dragged
him to the fair. Although there is precious little agricul-
ture and absolutely no industry on Nantucket, the big
event in those days was the annual Agricultural and In-
dustrial Fair. Something resembling a fourth-rate midway,
operated by sleazy-looking palefaces, always arrived from
the "continent" for the affair. There were a few so-called
thrill rides, crooked games of chance, improbable games
of skill, and a number of loud-mouthed jailbirds in straw
hats and purple shirts—with garters around the sleeves
—who would give you a cane worth a nickel if they failed
to guess your weight for a dime.

I wasn't allowed to go to the fair without an adult, and
that was how I happened to enlist the services of Chief
Nosoap.

He either had been or still was an official of the Boy
Scouts. At any rate, he was wearing his usual field-trip
garb of a broad-brimmed Scout hat, brown flannel shirt,
khaki knickers, wrap-around leggings of the doughboy
type, and high canvas sneakers which originally had been
white.

Smoking some evil aromatic mixture which gave out
orange-yellow fumes, he stayed well apart from the crowd
—or possibly it was the other way around—viewing the
antics with distasteful tolerance. When I tried to get him
to go on some of the rides with me, he grunted a firm

negative. But he pressed some change into my hand, slapped me across the seat of the pants, pointed to the rides, and told me to "Go." I thanked him and went.

I didn't even think about him again for half an hour or so. But then I heard a hubbub, and noticed a hurrah's-nest in front of one of the booths, with the ridiculous little figure of Chief Nosoap at the center of it. Not only that— he was surrounded by a heap of baby dolls, Mexican hats, riding whips, gilt bird cages, Indian blankets, plaster figurines, fancy lamps, and boxes of candy. And a Massachusetts State Trooper was hurrying majestically to his side.

I pushed my way through the crowd in time to hear the policeman ask our lighthouse guest, "Do you want to try your luck again, Professor?"

Chief Nosoap spotted me, winked a baseball-sized eye, and nodded an affirmative. He was holding a bow in one hand and three arrows in the other.

"For Crysake have a heart," pleaded a distraught carnival man from behind the counter of the booth. "Lookit what he's already won? I ain't hardly got no prizes left. I tell you, officer, this high old goat is ruining me."

"You've been taking money from these Nantucket people for two days," the State Trooper said loudly for the benefit of the crowd. "I been watching you. Now when you get somebody who can hit the balloons with an arrow, you don't want to play no more. Go ahead and shoot, Professor."

"I got to live, for Crysake," begged the carnival man. "The high old goat's a professional. Look, Buffalo Bill, go away, will you? Do you want to see me ruint?"

"Go ahead and shoot, Professor," said the policeman—and it was practically an order now.

Chief Nosoap shrugged, put a piece of wampum on the counter, winked again at me, and exhaled a cloud of sulphurous smoke which caused the crowd to fall back. Without bothering to take the pipe out of his mouth, he sent three arrows sailing one behind the other in quick succession toward the wall at the opposite end of the booth.

Pop-pop-pop, went three balloons, as the arrows quivered into the padded backboard.

"Ruint," moaned the carney man. "He ain't no amacher. He's a pro, for Crysake."

"Want to shoot again, Professor?" the Trooper asked hopefully.

But Chief Nosoap really didn't enjoy being the center of attraction, so he shook his head.

"You sure? I'll set you up." The policeman produced some wampum, but our guest shook his head again.

"All right, then. You're the boss," the Trooper conceded. "Give the Professor his prize," he ordered. "What will it be this time, Professor?"

The Chief looked at me, and I pointed toward a leather holster with a toy cowboy pistol. "Little stick make noise like thunder," I grinned.

"The pistol, please," translated Chief Nosoap.

"Give the kid the pistol," the policeman ordered. I strapped it on, and our guest and I picked up the rest of the loot and pushed our way through the grinning crowd.

Besides being a dead-eye archer, Chief Nosoap also had what seemed to be a sixth sense when it came to finding

Indian relics. He'd put himself in the shoes of an Indian—
only a minor transformation—and decide where the savage would have lived and hunted.

I suppose that the real reason he came to visit us was
because it gave him an opportunity to prowl around the
old camping grounds on the island. He surveyed the harbor for three or four days and made a couple of trips to
the Atheneum library. Then one morning we took our
row boat and rowed me across to Monomoy. We landed
there, walked a quarter of a mile up the harbor, and
stopped while Chief Nosoap sat on his haunches.

"They probably would camp *here*," he muttered more
to himself than to me. "And shot birds from behind that
dune. And dug clams off that point there. And if they
shot birds from behind the dune, the arrows should have
fallen right . . . Come along, boy."

We walked a couple of hundred yards, and then the
Chief stopped and turned over something with the toe of
a sneaker.

"There ought to be arrowheads here some place, boy,"
he said. "Why don't you look around and see if you can
find one?"

I looked down and found one right away. As a matter
of fact, it was the very object Chief Nosoap had turned
over with his sneaker. And before the morning was over,
I found two more arrowheads and a spearhead, all of
which I happened to pick up very near places at which
the Chief was standing.

"You've got eyes like an eagle, boy," he told me. "I
don't know what's the matter with me any more. I haven't
found a blessed thing!"

I've been back to that same spot several times, and subsequently I've been to a number of other Indian encampments. And since that day I've never found a blessed thing, either.

There were about 1,500 Indians living on Nantucket when the white men came. The Indians probably were of the Natick tribe—at any rate, they spoke the Natick language. Half of them lived on the eastern end of the island, and half on the western end. They used to kill off each other fairly regularly, until the son of a west-end chief married the daughter of an east-end chief. After that, an imaginary line was drawn down the middle of the island, and it was agreed that anyone who crossed the line on unfriendly business would be killed.

In the Natick language, "Nantucket" means "land far out at sea." The Indians believed that the giant god Moshup created Nantucket in a fit of anger. Moshup, they said, lived on Cape Cod where he sometimes pulled up trees by the roots and made big fires on which he broiled whales for supper. One night, becoming enraged because Cape Cod sand kept getting in his moccasins, he kicked them off and hurled them far out into the ocean. One of them became Nantucket and the other the neighboring island of Martha's Vineyard.

Envious Martha's Vineyard historians, who never have been able to forgive Nantucket for becoming the whaling capital of the world while the Vineyard remained a sand dune, have manufactured a different version of the legend. They say Moshup sat on the Vineyard and dumped the ashes of his pipe into the Atlantic, thus forming Nantucket. Also, they have the effrontery to allege that "Nantucket" doesn't really mean "land far out at sea" at all, but translates into "Devil's ash heap." Having invented an asinine legend, they thus also invent an asinine translation to support it.

But an impartial reader, I am sure, will realize that the zero of their legend added to the zero of their translation still produces zero. The only reason I bring up the matter at all is to demonstrate the extent to which uncontrollable jealousy can goad otherwise reliable scholars into falsifying the facts of history. Naturally, such falsifications make doubly difficult the task of truly impartial researchers who today seek to winnow the bright truth from the chaff of fabrications.

I might add, before leaving once and for all the touchy subject of Vineyard jealousy, that some rude Nantucketers have their own graphic if unprintable theory as to how the god-giant Moshup must have created Martha's Vineyard.

There can be little doubt, at any rate, concerning the legend as to how the Indians first settled Nantucket. Herman Melville, in his chapter entitled "Nantucket" in *Moby Dick* (which incidentally does *not* contain a chapter entitled "Martha's Vineyard") has given semi-official status to the legend.

"In olden times," writes Melville, "an eagle swooped down on the New England coast and carried off an infant Indian in his talons. With loud laments the parents saw the child borne out of sight over the wide waters. They resolved to follow in the same direction. Setting out in their canoes, after a perilous passage they discovered the island, and there they found an empty ivory casket—the poor little Indian's skeleton."

Leaving the legends and getting back to fact, Nantucket actually is a glacial deposit of sand and gravel. Shaped like a lamb chop and containing 30,000 acres, it is thirty miles south of the elbow of Cape Cod. The island is about fourteen miles long and three and a half miles wide, and no part of the United States along the Atlantic Coast lies so far from the mainland.

The Norsemen probably discovered Nantucket in the tenth century, but they were notoriously careless about keeping records. So the credit goes to an Englishman, Bartholomew Gosnold, who was searching for Virginia in 1602 —the year before Queen Elizabeth died. Gosnold sailed the Atlantic in a small bark, and made a landfall at Nantucket's Sankaty Head, a cliff where a tall lighthouse now stands. On that same voyage he also discovered Cape Cod, which he named for the codfish swimming almost solidly around his ship.

Since the Virgin Queen had the lucrative policy of claiming for herself all virgin territory discovered by her subjects, Nantucket was deemed to belong automatically to the British crown. In 1635 Charles I—he's the king who specialized in Star Chamber trials, dissolved Parliament, persecuted Puritans, and eventually was beheaded—ordered his Plymouth Company to convey the island to William Alexander, Earl of Sterling. The Earl, in turn, sold Nantucket, Martha's Vineyard, and a good deal of other land that he owned to Thomas Mayhew and his "sonne," Thomas Jr., in 1641 for forty pounds. To sew up his title, Mayhew also paid some money to Sir Ferdinando Gorges,

Lord Proprietor of Maine, who claimed Nantucket. Then, being one of the few white men who believed that the Indians had a claim to their land, Mayhew bought the sachem rights to a large portion of Nantucket from the Indian chiefs there.

Mayhew was a Puritan Watertown merchant, and he and his son set out to make good Christians of the Indians on Martha's Vineyard and Nantucket. Thomas Jr. established the first white settlement on Martha's Vineyard in 1642. They translated the Bible into Natick language, and were so kind and understanding in their treatment of the Indians that they made many converts. Their dealings with the Indians might well have been—but certainly weren't—a pattern for all American pioneers.

The younger Mayhew sailed for England in 1657 to solicit funds for their missionary work, but the ship was lost with all hands. Broken-hearted, his father decided to sell their lands.

So Nantucket was on the real-estate market, and it was bought in 1659 by nine New Englanders, most of whom were living at Salisbury, in the Massachusetts Bay Colony. The price was "thirty pounds and two bever hatts." One "hatt" was for old Mayhew himself, the other for his wife.

The nine were Tristram Coffin, Thomas Macy, Christopher Hussey, Richard Swain, Thomas Barnard, Peter Coffin, Stephen Greenleaf, John Swain, and William Pile. Each of them took a partner.

Tristram Coffin was the moving spirit of the venture, and is considered the father of Nantucket. Four generations later, he had fifteen hundred descendants! But the credit for establishing the first settlement on Nantucket

goes to another of the nine purchasers—Thomas Macy, an
ancestor of R. H. Macy, founder of the New York department store. Thomas Macy, his wife, Sarah, their five children, a widower named Edward Starbuck, and a twelve-
year-old orphan, Isaac Coleman, sailed from the "continent" to Nantucket in the autumn of 1659.

They made the trip in Macy's small, open sloop, and it
was a wet, rough journey which Mrs. Macy didn't enjoy
in the least. As the Macy boat approached Madaket, on
the western tip of Nantucket, the Indians gathered ex-
citedly on the shore. The savages, whooping greetings,
scared Mrs. Macy so thoroughly that she wanted to turn
back. And the baby had "fitts." But Macy himself—having
invested somewhat more than three pounds in the island,
not to mention his share of the cost of the two "bever
hatts"—was determined to land. Consequently, he ordered
Sarah to hush herself and the baby, to keep a stiff upper
lip, and "to seek thy God."

"I fear not the witches on earth nor the devils in hell,"
he is recorded as saying, while he guided the boat toward
the posturing redskins on the beach.

The Indians, remembering the kindnesses of the May-
hews, greeted the first settlers hospitably. They helped
them build a shack at Madaket, where the whites spent
the winter. The Indians showed them where to dig for the
best clams, and how to catch bass and bluefish in the surf
along the South Shore. The Indians didn't know it, but in
spite of their kindnesses they were signing their death
warrants.

The next summer, 1660, ten more families moved from
Salisbury and vicinity to Nantucket. They settled at Ca-

paum Harbor, on the North Shore, near the site of the present watertower—the first landfall now as one approaches Nantucket by steamer.

The new settlement was named Sherburne on April 18, 1673, by Francis Lovelace, governor of New York. In 1692, at the request of the settlers, the British Parliament took the island away from New York and gave it to Massachusetts. For some reason which is beyond me, New York didn't complain and I find no record that Massachusetts rejoiced. About 1700, a storm threw a bank of sand across the entrance to Capaum Harbor, making the harbor an inland pond. As a result of this, the settlers started moving to a point three or four miles southeast, on a larger and much more sheltered harbor, where the community really should have been located in the first place. That's where the town of Nantucket is now. The name of Sherburne was changed to Nantucket in 1795.

So much for vital statistics. But why did the original white settlers leave their friends and the comparative comforts of the mainland? "What sought they thus afar," on a barren and isolated island? That question never has been fully answered. There is even some doubt as to how barren Nantucket really *was* back in those days.

Obed Macy, a descendant of the first settler, Thomas Macy, wrote an authoritative *History of Nantucket* in 1835. Obed concedes that, in his day, Nantucket was void of trees and had a soil which he could not conscientiously "rate above middling." When a Nantucketer can't give a grade above "middling" to something on his own sacred island, you can be pretty sure that an impartial judge "from off" would grade it as hopeless.

But Historian Macy goes on to say that when his ancestor Thomas arrived on the island, there were forests of big trees and the soil was lush—so lush that Ebenezer Barnard, "a man of strict veracity," reported in 1729 that he had made fifty bushels of corn to the acre. Historian Macy explains that the early settlers ruined the soil by cutting the trees and by unwise plowing.

Quite different evidence is offered in *Moby Dick*, written in 1851. Herman Melville said the original settlers found Nantucket so bare they even had "to plant weeds there."

And as for there being any sort of forests, Melville says there wasn't a blessed tree on the whole island, and that the first settlers treasured scraps of wood "like bits of the true cross in Rome." In fact, he adds, the settlers had to "plant toadstools before their houses, to get under the shade in summertime," and grass was so rare that "one blade . . . is an oasis; three blades a walk in the prairie."

Of course, Melville had his tongue in cheek. But I don't think that what he says can be completely discounted. All I can personally vouch for is the condition of Nantucket today. I shall be truthful and, I hope, diplomatic: While the island is not exactly barren, neither is it a Sequoia National Forest or a San Joaquin Valley. If beach grass counts as grass, there's quite a bit of it.

Certainly one reason that the original settlers moved to Nantucket was because they couldn't stand the terrible bossiness of witch-burning leaders of the Massachusetts Bay Colony.

Thomas Macy—the first settler, not the historian—was

in trouble with the Massachusetts officials about a religious matter, when he decided to leave for Nantucket. Macy's trouble stemmed from the fact that he had given shelter to four Quakers, who had stopped at his Salisbury house during a heavy rainstorm.

To let a Quaker come into a house, no matter how hard it was raining, was a violation of a Massachusetts law passed in 1655. This law described the Quakers as "a cursed sect of hereticks lately risen up in the world, who take upon them to speake & write blasphemous opinions, despising government & the order of God." Quakers themselves were to be sentenced to death, the law said, and persons who harbored them were to be fined and whipped.

Macy, a Baptist and an Englishman by birth, escaped with a minor fine and no whipping, when he wrote the court that the Quakers had stayed in his house for only three-quarters of an hour.

"They spoke not many words in the time and neither was I at leisure to talk with them; for I came home wet to the skine and I found my wife sick in bed," he added.

His letter to the court is dated August 27, 1659, and shortly after that, Macy left for Nantucket.

John Greenleaf Whittier, the Quaker poet, wrote in *The Exile* about 1840 that Macy dramatically *escaped* from Salisbury to Nantucket, after harboring the Quakers. Whittier says that while the Quakers were in "Goodman" Macy's house, ten or twelve horsemen including a Puritan minister rode up to the door and shouted:

> Now Goodman Macy, ope thy door,
> We would not be house-breakers;

> A rueful deed thou's done this day,
> In harboring banished Quakers.

While the horsemen seized the Quakers, Whittier continues, Macy and his wife raced to the shore, leaped into his boat, and shoved off. The Puritan minister was hot on their heels.

> "Come back! come back!" the parson cried,
> "The church's curse beware."
> "Curse, an thou wilt," said Macy, "but
> Thy blessings prithee spare."

That makes a dramatic story, but it doesn't account for the Macys' rounding up five children and the other two passengers. Court records clearly indicate that Macy wasn't forced to depart in haste, and that his trip was carefully planned. Whittier, although the sort of poet who rhymed "house-breakers" and "Quakers," was still a much better poet than he was an historian.

Religious persecution certainly was a factor, although not a governing one, in the settling of Nantucket. It should be borne in mind that—regardless of the high-sounding assertions of certain idealistic historians—the Massachusetts Puritans hadn't come to the New World to establish religious freedom. True enough, they had left England because of the *lack* of religious freedom, which prevented them from worshiping in their own way. But the purpose of their pilgrimage was to establish and enforce their own religion, not to found a colony in which every man could worship as he pleased. There was far less religious freedom in Massachusetts than in England.

The large majority of the persons who migrated from

the mainland to Nantucket, however, weren't motivated
by religious matters. They moved to the island simply because they believed they would prosper there and have
"butter on the pie," which is the Nantucket equivalent of
the Southern phrase, "live high on the hog." Most of the
first settlers intended to—and actually did—raise sheep
on the island. And in spite of Melville's remarks, there was
adequate grazing for sheep on the Nantucket "commons,"
now known as the moors.

If any of the first settlers thought that by moving to
Nantucket they were freeing their descendants from religious bossiness, they made a terrible mistake. For Nantucket was to become a Quaker island. And while the
Quakers didn't burn witches or candles-at-both-ends, they
were probably the bossiest and nosiest people who ever
lived.

Whatever the individual reasons for migration, the settlers soon started to populate the island by raising hordes
of children. And those children—one of whom grew up to
be Benjamin Franklin's mother—and *their* children soon
caused the world to sit up and take notice.

But as the whites increased, the Indians decreased. Now-
adays, with a feeling of self-guilt, we are inclined to blame
our ancestors for the degradation and elimination of the
Redmen, but the fact is that no one was to blame.

The history of red and white race relations on Nantucket portrays in capsule form the whole dilemma. The
early settlers on Nantucket were basically good people
who made an honest attempt to live with the Indians and
improve their way of life. There was no warfare. But the
once self-sufficient Indians became drunken, no-good loaf-

ers, just the same. The only way the colonists could possibly have solved the "Indian problem" would have been to sail back to Europe. Even today, with the benefit of hindsight, it is difficult to see how the white and red cultures could be successfully mixed.

As long as the Indians had to take care of themselves or die, they got along all right. If a tribe didn't raise enough corn to feed itself, some members starved to death. No Indian worried much about that, because human life was held cheap, and the dead were probably better off, anyway, in the Happy Hunting Ground.

But when the white people came to Nantucket, they simply couldn't sit back and watch an Indian's family starve during the winter—starve because the father and his squaw had been too lazy to plant corn the year before.

So the white people would give the Indians food to tide them over the winter. And then, when spring came, *no* Indian wanted to plant corn. What was the use of planting corn, the Indians reasoned, when the white men would feed you if you were hungry? The white men, exasperated, told the Indians they *had* to plant corn. When the Indians wouldn't obey, they were arrested and brought to trial. But you couldn't fine an Indian for breaking a law, because he didn't own anything with which to pay the fine. And you couldn't put every Indian in jail, because then all the whites would be working to feed all the Indians— which would have suited the Indians very well.

Consequently, under court order, Indians who wouldn't work were whipped. Of course that was brutal and it caused great resentment. But it is easy to understand how the whites justified the whippings: "If they don't work, they'll starve to death. We, as good Christians, can't sit back and let them starve. Therefore we must make them work. And the only way the cussed savages will work is when they are whipped."

The settlers were careful—at the beginning—to leave the Indians enough land so they could support themselves. But the settlers figured that they, too, had to have land to support *themselves*. This land was duly bought from the Indians—maybe at bargain prices, but nevertheless bought. The trouble was the Indians didn't understand that when a man owned land, he could prevent others from using it. An Indian thought that land, like air, belonged to everyone. Since he didn't grasp or approve the white man's law against trespass, the Indian was always in trouble for grazing his horse in some settler's prize corn field or for housebreaking.

Also, when it came to community improvement projects, the Indians refused to cooperate at all. There was one occasion, for instance, when the whites decided a pond should be drained for health reasons and to obtain fish. Every able-bodied man was supposed to help dig the necessary ditch. But when the Indians were assigned a certain number of man-hours on the ditch, they balked. If the white men wanted to drain a pond, said the Indians, let the white men drain it. The Indians were satisfied with the pond just as it was.

But of course when the white men *did* drain the pond, the Indians wanted their share of the fish.

Finally, and probably most importantly, there was the matter of liquor. When the Indians got their first taste of rum, they found it wonderful medicine which made every

brave a chief. Most of them decided to spend the rest of
their lives drinking. When liquor was denied them, they
broke into buildings and stole it. When guards were placed
around the buildings, the Indians bashed in the guards'
heads.

Understandably, the whites got more and more exasperated. It wasn't very pleasant to be penned up on an
island with 1,500 impossible dipsomaniacs who would steal
and murder to get a bottle of rum, and then drink themselves into a war-whooping frenzy.

Yet, the Indians weren't really to blame for their troubles, because the troubles wouldn't even have existed if it
hadn't been for the settlers. The whole point is, as I've
mentioned, that no one was to blame.

Judged by Puritan standards, the Indian was—or soon
became—an irresponsible, shiftless, immoral sinner. The
Nantucket settlers, never noted for minding their own business, thought it was their "Christian Duty" to make Indians behave like Puritans. The Indians pointed out, quite
logically but to no avail, that they were there first; that
they weren't trying to make Puritans behave like Indians;
and that the least their visitors could do was to leave them
alone.

Court records are testimony of meddlesome efforts by
the settlers to improve the morals of the Indians. For instance, here is a sample decision in a case of squaw-
desertion:

"Nakattactonnit must take again his wife and live love-
ingly with her or else he shall be severely whipped. Also,
Nahkaquetan, the woman that the aforesaid Indian hath
kept company with shall be whipt Ten Stripe."

Of course, the Indians formerly had had their own ways of settling disputes. But now when they found out they weren't supposed to fight and kill each other any more, they became intrigued by the white men's courts. The Indians started hundreds of inane suits against the white men—but never got any place—and also dragged each other into court on the most trivial of grounds.

Things began to get hopelessly mixed up when the white man's legal and moral codes were applied to Indian customs. For instance, there was the case of Chief Wauwinet's son, who was given the proper Christian name of Isaac but who nevertheless was known to the Indians as Nicornoose, which means Sucker of the Fore Teat (a free translation, I think, would be Lucky Boy.)

Nicornoose married and had a son and a daughter, and then he kicked out his wife and started living with another squaw, by whom he had two sons.

Nicornoose's oldest and legitimate son got so angry at his father for taking the new squaw that he moved off the island in a huff. And some sixty years later, one of his sons —Nicornoose's grandson—returned to Nantucket and said that *he*—instead of Nicornoose's illegitimate descendants —was entitled under the white man's law to the sachem rights which dated back to Wauwinet. Meanwhile, the white men had bought the sachem rights from Sucker of the Fore Teat's illegitimate descendants, and so the whites had to buy off his legitimate grandson.

Cases of Indian against Indian completely clogged the court docket around about 1700. The settlers in desperation established an Indian court, headed by a brave named Esquire Kadooda.

Esquire soon became just about as lazy as his fellow Indians, and he disliked all of the work made necessary by his crowded docket. So he began a practice known as "Kadooda's law."

Whenever two Indians appeared before him with a complaint, Esquire would order them both to be soundly whipped. Then, after the whippings, he'd hear their evidence against each other. As soon as the word of "Kadooda's law" got around, his docket was considerably lightened, and Esquire could take life easy.

Syphilis and other diseases killed off Indians by the hundreds, and many others died of alcoholism. In 1763, when there were only 358 Indians left on Nantucket, a brig from Ireland was wrecked on the North Shore. Some Indians helped rescue the crew and several members of the crew were suffering from a disease that may have been yellow fever. At any rate, the disease swept through the Indian population and killed 222 of the 358. For some reason, white Nantucketers were immune to this plague.

The last full-blooded Indian brave on Nantucket died in 1822. And the last man of Indian blood, Abram Quary, died Nov. 25, 1854. He was eighty-two years old.

A painting of Mr. Quary, sitting barefoot and alone in his cabin, hangs in the Atheneum library. It's a sad, lonesome scene—and I suppose that's the way the artist meant it to be. The old Indian, with hands folded in his lap, is blankly contemplating his knees. And as a final mark of his shoeless domestication, a kettle hangs on a crane in the fireplace for a cup of tea.

Poor Abram Quary! His painting and some arrowheads, bone fishhooks, and the like are all that are left of a people who had lived on Nantucket for countless centuries and who would be alive today if it weren't for all of us.

Many of the mainland Indians died in proud, savage fury while swinging tomahawks against the despised white spoilers. The hospitable Nantucket Indians died on the beaches in alcoholic stupors when the tides came in; died from racking coughs and high fever in their filthy huts and wigwams.

If it is important how a man dies, as well as how he lives, the Nantucket Indians should have thrown a warning spear across the bow of Thomas Macy's sloop, and then put on their war paint and prepared to defend the island to the last brave.

3. WITH BIBLE AND HARPOON

My father could take in stride—which only occasionally faltered—the necessary expenses of feeding and clothing us. But he drew the line at any sort of waste, and he wanted to be sure that we were brought up to think that waste was wicked.

Dad made his living by saving time for industry—he was a consulting engineer in motion study and management. And to teach us not to be idle during periods of what he called "unavoidable delay," he painted messages in Morse Code on the dormitory ceilings and the bathroom walls of our Nantucket cottage.

The messages themselves were unimportant, but Dad thought it would be good mental exercise for us to learn the code.

"The point is that you want to get into the habit of

keeping your mind busy, even when you're brushing your teeth or lying down in bed," he used to tell us. "You don't ever want to waste a minute, in training your mind."

When it came to money, Dad sometimes could tolerate our big expenses better than the little ones. For instance, if one of the girls bought an expensive pair of shoes—and the shoes had low heels and toes round enough so they didn't cramp the feet—he'd concede that good workmanship could be expected to cost money. But if the shoes, no matter how inexpensive, had high heels and pointed toes, he'd complain feelingly about how his ultimate destination was Our Island Home, the Nantucket poorhouse.

The "waste" that irritated Dad more than any other was the needless burning of electric bulbs. He came from a generation which had relied on kerosene lamps and gas mantles, and the fact that electricity was a much cheaper form of illumination made no difference when it came to the principle of wasting light.

He'd make the rounds of our cottage, before he sat down at the supper table, and if he found so much as one light burning in an empty room he'd lecture us gloomily on the importance of thrift and on the precarious state of the family's finances.

"I found lights burning tonight in the boys' dormitory *and* the girls' dormitory," he'd sigh. "Oh, well, what's the use. I'd better drop by Our Island Home and see if I can make a reservation."

One of my older sisters, who was good at arithmetic and was also one of the worst offenders when it came to forgetting about lights, thought it might cheer up Dad if she could convince him that the waste wasn't really so gigantic. So she dropped by the utility company and got some figures on rates and the amount of electricity which the average bulb consumed.

"Never mind, Dad," she told him brightly when he informed her that she hadn't turned out a light. "That room hasn't been empty for more than five minutes, so the very most it could cost you is about a tenth of a cent."

"That means we could leave *ten* lights on, and it wouldn't cost you any more than a penny, doesn't it, Daddy?" one of the young boys asked. "Gosh, what's a measly old penny, eh Daddy? I've got a lot of them in my bank, so you won't have to go to Our Island Home for awhile yet."

Dad usually was extremely pleased when his children showed a facility in arithmetic, but on this particular occasion neither the knowledge about the tenth of a cent nor the additional knowledge about ten for a penny seemed to cause any elation.

"Some people apparently think that tenths of a cent grow on trees," was the best he could come up with, while he glowered at my sister. "And since some people have so many pennies in their bank," he added darkly to my young brother, "from now on we'll have a system of fines around here. Anyone who leaves a light burning will be fined a penny."

"Aw, who cares about a measly old penny, eh Daddy?" asked the young brother. "I got a lot of them . . ."

"I know," Dad interrupted. "You've got altogether too many of them for your own good, if you ask me. Well, you won't have them long and you'll see a poor man's face in the mirror for the rest of your life, if you don't learn not to waste things like electricity."

When it came to putting out lights, Dad and the early Nantucket Quakers had a great deal in common. Although the Quakers shipped whale oil around the world, they had a phobia against wasting it. "Two lamps burning and no ship at sea" was the sneering phrase applied on Nantucket to anyone who made a bright show of prosperity by living above his income.

In the old days, Nantucket streets were so pitch black that visitors who ventured out on moonless nights almost invariably got lost. In fact, India Street got its name because even islanders themselves had to admit it was "dark as India."

When people from off island asked why there weren't any street-lights the Quakers had two different answers —depending on the world price of whale oil. If the price were high, the Quakers said that they naturally wanted to sell all their "ile" while the market was up. And if the price were low, they said they had to sell every drop they could get their hands on, to make ends meet.

In fact, Nantucket Quakers were probably the thriftiest people who ever lived on the face of the earth. They saved everything, including words and syllables. They often referred to Nantucket as 'Tucket, and Siasconset became 'Sconset. Anyone from off island was known simply as "from off," and spermaceti whale oil was shortened to sperm.

This habit of saving everything explains why it is possible today to get such an accurate picture of Nantucket whaling. Instead of throwing away their old log books, the Quaker captains gave them to their wives and children to use as scrapbooks. Only recently, Mr. Edouard A. Stackpole, the writer and historian, advertised in *The Nantucket Inquirer and Mirror* that he would buy old scrapbooks. As a result of the ad, he obtained eight or ten scrapbooks, six of which proved to be old logs on which recipes, pressed flowers, and newspaper clippings had been pasted. One of the logs happened to be that of the Nantucket schooner *Huntress*, captained by Christopher Burdick, and contained information proving the claim that American sealhunters in 1821 were the first to recognize Antarctica as a continent.

Whaling and Quakerism came to Nantucket at about the same time, and it's difficult to say which was the more important. Whales brought money to Nantucket, and the Quakers saw to it that the money was wisely invested. The Quakers also bred men ideally suited by temperament to captain whaling vessels.

Besides being tightfisted, the Quaker was a glum, sanctimonious, nosey, meddlesome killjoy. If anything was fun, he was against it. If it was pretty, he covered it. If it was natural, he suppressed it. If it was musical, he silenced it. If it was artistic, he suspected it.

I'm talking about the Nantucket Quakers, not the Philadelphia variety. While the Philadelphia Quaker certainly was no free-spending playboy, he never entirely lost his perspective.

But on Nantucket, where there was little direct contact with the outside world, Quakerism reached monumental extremes before it finally expired from its own bossy excesses. No people would put up indefinitely with a religion which uprooted flowers because they were worldly and which sent delegations of tight-lipped, scissor-bearing busybodies into the homes of erring members to snip decorative tassels from lampshades.

Yet, before Quakerism died on Nantucket, it fathered an amazing society which might have stepped right out of the pages of *Poor Richard's Almanack.*

Truth, honesty, craftmanship, industry, plainness of dress, and sobriety were all part of the Nantucketers' religion. Solely because of these traits, Nantucket overcame the obstacles of isolation and shallow harbor to become the one place on earth where whaleships could best be fitted for sea. And although Quakers opposed violence and bloodshed, they became unexcelled at the goriest, riskiest, most thrilling, and most violent occupation of the day—hunting whales.

The almost unbelievable courage of the Quakers was a source of both amazement and irritation to the rest of the world. In fact the very name "Quaker" was coined because the original English Friends refused to quake in the face of cruel religious persecution, and instead had the effrontery to advise their persecutors to start quaking.

George Fox, the English weaver's son who established the Society of Friends in England eleven years before Nantucket was settled, spent a good deal of time in British jails as a heretic. But when various judges ordered him to change his religious views, he shook a fateful finger in their scared faces and told them in a voice of doom that if they knew what was good for them, they'd better "quake and tremble at the word of the Lord." He made a good many converts that way, too. The most prominent English Quaker, of course, was William Penn.

When the Quakers started proselyting in America, the Massachusetts Puritans quickly decided that the best way to get rid of them was to hang them. However, despite their witch-burning background, the Puritans didn't feel entirely right about hanging lady Quakers. So in the case of Mary Dyer, a Quaker from Rhode Island, that posed quite a problem. No matter how often she was warned, Mary kept journeying from Providence to Boston, to try to make Friends. The authorities in Boston would arrest her, threaten her, humiliate her, and ship her back to Providence. But they couldn't intimidate her, and in a few weeks she'd be back in Boston trying to convert Puritans into Quakers.

Finally, the Massachusetts authorities decided that they'd better try some psychology on Mary, before she ran them crazy. So when she arrived in Boston late in 1659 —the same year that Thomas Macy settled on Nantucket —the authorities arrested her and sentenced her to death.

It so happened that two of the Quakers who had stopped during a rainstorm at Thomas Macy's house in Salisbury had subsequently been arrested, and also had been sentenced to death. Their names were Marmaduke Stevenson and William Robinson, both from England. They were in the same Boston jail as Mary—and the Massachusetts authorities didn't have any qualms about hanging Quaker men.

One autumn day, to the beat of rolling drums, Stevenson, Robinson, and Mary Dyer were marched to the gallows with an escort of a hundred troops.

Stevenson was hanged. Then Robinson was hanged. And finally Mary Dyer, erect and unafraid, stood on the scaffold above the dangling bodies. They tied her hands and placed a noose around her neck, and still she didn't quake.

Then they told her she had been reprieved—if only she would please, please, please go back to Providence and this time stay there! Or if she didn't want to stay there, at least to keep out of Boston. Because next time she wouldn't get off so easily—they'd hang her just as sure as she was alive.

They escorted Mary to Rhode Island, all right, but they couldn't keep her there. Although her family begged her to stay home, she was back in Boston again within three months, trying to convert Puritans to Quakers. Again she was arrested and sentenced to be hanged. Again she was marched to the gallows, where her hands were tied and a noose placed around her neck. But this time, the not unlimited patience of the Massachusetts authorities had been exhausted. There was no reprieve, and the hangman did his duty.

About thirty years after that, Quaker "missionaries" started coming to Nantucket. Although they weren't persecuted, they didn't make much headway until 1701, when an English Friend named John Richardson managed to convert Mrs. Mary Coffin Starbuck. And largely because of that one conversion, Nantucket was a Quaker town for 150 years!

Mrs. Starbuck didn't hold any official position in Nantucket, but she was unquestionably the queen bee of the island, where she was known as "The Great Woman."

For one thing, she was the daughter of Tristram Coffin, the Father of Nantucket. For another, she herself was one of the original settlers and had married the well-to-do Nathaniel Starbuck. And for a third, she and Nathaniel were the parents of the first white child born on the island.

With wealth, the right family connections, and the right pioneer background, Mrs. Starbuck was the social leader of the community and lived in the finest house. And she was respected, too, because of her common sense and the untiring work she had done to improve the conditions of the Indians.

Now Nantucket women were well ahead of the rest of the colonies in securing "women's rights." An island woman had to do a man's chores when he was away at sea. And once she got accustomed to running things in his absence, she didn't take too much nonsense from him when he was home. The record of Captain Benjamin Worth shows that the men's absences were prolonged. Captain Worth was home a total of only six years during the forty-one years he was a whaler. Incidentally, he brought home 19,000 barrels of "ile," sailed 879,960 miles and never lost a man!

But many men *were* lost at sea, so the ratio of widows and spinsters was high. At about the time that Mrs. Starbuck became a Quaker, the women on the island outnumbered the men by four to one. And a stock joke among the bachelor girls, who professed not to envy their married sisters, was that it took a mighty good husband to be better than none.

Many of the widows and spinsters found it necessary to make a living and opened shops. The resulting petticoat aristocrocy caused many a henpecked sea captain to cut short his "vacation" at home.

A Frenchman-turned-Pennsylvanian, who visited Nantucket in the eighteenth century, was impressed by this petticoat rule, almost unprecedented elsewhere in the world. In his *Letters from an American Farmer*, J. Hector St. John de Crèvecoeur wrote of Nantucketers:

". . . their wives, in their absence, are necessarily obliged to transact business, to settle accounts, and in short to rule and provide for their families. . . . This employment ripens their judgment and justly entitles them to a rank superior to that of other wives. . . . The men at their return . . . cheerfully give their consent to every transaction that has happened in their absence, and all is joy and peace. . . . 'Wife, thee hast done well,' is the general approbation they receive."

The first Quaker meetings were held in Mrs. Starbuck's house, and the first Friends' Meeting House was built in 1711, at the southeast of the settlers' first burial grounds. Within a few years, about half the Nantucketers—including virtually all the best families, the temperance leaders, and the petticoat aristocracy; the blue-bloods, blue-noses, and blue-stockings—were Quakers.

The Society of Friends had no paid ministers. In fact the wags among the "Nothingarians"—a small group of islanders who stubbornly refused to belong to any church at all—used to cackle rudely that the reason so many of their tight-fisted neighbors had embraced the Quaker faith was because they didn't have to pay ministers' salaries.

Actually, the sternness and integrity of Quakerism was ready-made for the pioneers on Nantucket. There's no denying, either, that the faith was ideally suited to the thrifty father who wanted his family to economize: No fancy clothes, no gay parties, no idle amusements. Quaker boys were supposed to start making their own living long before they were grown. They often went to sea at the age of twelve, under the guidance of some uncle or cousin who was a sea-captain. Quaker girls, no matter how wealthy, were supposed to sew and help with the housework almost as soon as they were old enough to walk.

Armed with Bibles and harpoons, Quaker sea captains were formidable figures whose love of money was exceeded—or perhaps "tied" would be a more accurate verb —only by their love of the Lord. No one ever drove a harder bargain or stuck to the bargain with more integrity.

For example, there's a story about a harpooner on a whaleship out of Nantucket who once made the mistake of absently driving his weapon into a beam of the ship. The beam wasn't damaged, but the Quaker captain saw an opportunity to teach the crew a lesson about respecting property, and at the same time to increase the revenue of the owners. So he told the harpooner that he'd have to pay for the beam, and that the cost would be deducted from his "lay"—the share of the voyage's profits.

The harpooner knew better than to complain, so he bided his time until the ship had returned to Nantucket and was fitted out for another voyage. He didn't sign on for the new voyage, but a few hours before the ship was to sail he came aboard carrying a crowbar and a wicked-looking axe.

"With thy permission," he told the captain, "I have come to get my beam."

The captain knew he was outsmarted, and finally had to buy back the beam at the price he had charged the harpooner, plus six per cent interest.

Good Quakers never cursed, and many Quaker captains were as religious afloat as they were ashore. It's pretty well documented, though, that some of the captains had non-Quaker mates "from off," who did their swearing for them. That was the case on Captain Cromwell Barnard's ship, and it stood him in good stead one time, when he ran into some trouble at a dock in Philadelphia.

An incoming ship wanted to berth too close to Barnard's vessel, and the captain of the incoming ship wouldn't pay any attention to the mild old Nantucketer.

So Barnard finally stuck his head into the officers' mess and said regretfully:

"Mate, I think thee'll have to come up here and use some of thy language."

The mate, a burly, unshaved mainlander, came roaring to the quarter-deck and uncorked a string of unprintable expletives, larded generously with irreverent references to the Father, Son, and Holy Ghost.

"Thee has a useful talent, Mate," Captain Barnard conceded reluctantly as the other ship hastily veered away.

One Nantucket spinster was secretly in love with an off-island mate and had hopes of reforming him. Just before his ship sailed, she wrapped up a Bible, took it to the wharf, and gave it to him.

"Thankee for the package, Miss," he enthused. "I won't

open it until we've cleared Brant Point. Is there anything breakable in it?"

"Only the Ten Commandments," she told him tartly.

Some Quaker captains wouldn't "lower" for a whale on Sunday, even if it was the first they had sighted in more than a year of hunting. There was one extremist who wouldn't even allow his lookouts to report whales on Sundays. His crew said, though, that despite his great show of ignoring Sabbath whales, the ship never seemed to be very far away from the prey when first-light broke Monday morning.

Of course there were some skippers who were "shore saints, sea devils"—pillars of the church at home and foul-mouthed sadists afloat. They might read the Bible aloud in fatherly tones to the assembled crew, and then order that some youngster suffering from "Cape Horn fever," as malingering was called, be given a dose of belaying pin hash or a taste of the cat.

One shore saint, sea devil returned to Nantucket in a black mood, without a drop of oil. The owners, who belonged to the same Quaker Meeting House as the captain, boarded the ship as she came up to the dock. Eagerly, they asked him what sort of luck he had had.

"For three blanketty-blank years," roared the captain, sputtering out profanity that curled the hawsers, "I've combed the unprintable Pacific without so much as seeing one single, illegitimate, censored, related-to-a dog, stinking whale."

Then suddenly remembering himself, he lowered his voice and added unctuously in dignified, Quaker tones,

"But I'm glad to report to thee that we had an extremely pleasant sail."

Most of the Nantucket captains were strait-laced, able, and considerate of their crews. But of course it's the exceptions that cause notice. I've come across one log-book which records that the captain died of delirium tremens. Before he passed away, though, he ordered all hands aloft and then took potshots at them with his revolver. Fortunately, he was too drunk to bag any human game. Another skipper, a gorilla-like man who thought his mate talked too much, gagged that officer by shoving a belaying pin down his throat.

Also, a few Quaker captains didn't behave as they should with the chesty, light-skinned beauties of Polynesia. One captain had an uninhibited, dusky wife and a gay brood of children in the South Seas, whom he visited on every voyage, and an inhibited, Quaker wife and solemn brood of children back home at Nantucket.

Certainly it is understandable that to a proper Quaker—who had never seen his wife or any other woman when she wasn't all bundled up in form-hiding clothes or nightdress—the first sight of a languid, naked South Sea Island belle, with a flower in her hair, must have been a pleasant shock.

At home at Nantucket, the Quaker influence was an iron hand. England's pleasure-loving King Charles II—who had no legitimate children but fathered a bumper crop of illegitimate ones, including two sons by Actress Nell Gwyn—had been dead for sixteen years when Quakerism came to Nantucket. But the filigree styles of his reign lived on, and it was perhaps in rebellion against these styles that the Quakers insisted on gloomy, functional clothes.

Men's suits were severely cut, and usually of gray or brown homespun. Square-toed shoes were the trademark of Quaker men. Women wore plain and shapeless dresses, which hung tent-like from neck to ankles. The women further hid the contours of their torsos with blanket-sized shawls, and the trademark of a Quaker woman was a "scuttle" bonnet—shaped like an inverted coal-scuttle—which hid all of her hair and most of her face. A man couldn't recognize his wife or his sister on the street, unless he happened to come up to her bows on.

Because buttons were suspect as a form of needless decoration, they were largely replaced by hooks and eyes. Even men's coats and trousers were held together with these metal fasteners.

Crèvecoeur wrote that only on "First Day"—Sunday—were the Friends permitted to wear clothes imported from England, and "even these are of the most moderate price and of the gravest colours. There is no kind of difference in their dress; they are all clad alike, and resemble in that respect the members of one family."

The Friends called the days of the week "First Day," "Second Day," and so forth, because they didn't approve of the names of pagan gods associated with the days. In the Nantucket schools, the teachers even referred to Robinson Crusoe's colored companion as his "Man Sixth Day."

They always used "thee" and "thou" because, in the seventeenth century, some pronouns could be employed in such a way as to imply differences in social classes. An

Englishman, for instance, might address his equal in the second person as "you," and his superior in the third person as "his lordship," or "his highness."

On First Day, the Friends assembled in gloomy, unheated Meeting Houses, where they would sit in meditative silence until someone was moved to speak. Although there were no ministers, many Quakers became fluent and moving religious lecturers. Women had as much right to speak as men, and were given equal attention. Sometimes the speeches would deal acidly with infractions of the Quaker code of morals. Since specific names and specific instances were mentioned, the women so singled out for specific attention must have been thankful for the face-hiding scuttle bonnets.

Select committees of the Meeting, appointed to oversee the "good of the order," patrolled Nantucket and checked on such tabooed matters as dancing, card-playing, swearing, hand-holding, singing, flower-growing, and wearing gaily colored clothes. A person suspected of any of these offenses was placed immediately "under dealings." This meant he would be visited at home by a stern and official delegation of Friends, who would cross-question him and point out the error of his ways.

Persons who didn't pay their bills, who lived above their incomes, or who failed to fulfill contracts also were visited by select committees.

If a person "under dealings" didn't turn over a new leaf after he was "precautioned" and "labored with" by a select committee, he would be summoned to appear at Meeting, before the whole congregation. If he refused to appear or if, after his appearance, the congregation decided he wasn't a good Friend, he would be "disowned" and "set aside."

Maria Mitchell, the famous Nantucket astronomer, got her father into serious trouble when she brought a piano into their house. Mr. Mitchell was placed under dealings and Maria herself subsequently—but not because of the piano—was disowned.

A merchant who made the mistake of appearing one day in shoes with silver buckles was immediately disowned. To associate with "World's People"—non-Quakers —was a serious offense. To marry one of them meant being automatically set aside, and even to attend a wedding of non-Quakers was forbidden, and meant big dealings. One young man was disowned because he wore his hair tied in a knot. A young widow who planted a wild rose bush over her husband's otherwise unmarked grave was instructed to cut it down.

When two Friends wanted to marry, and thus presumably become very good friends, they first were required to declare their intentions, at Meeting. Then an all-male committee was appointed to "inspect" the character of the would-be bridegroom, and an all-female committee to do the same for the bride.

While the marriage was "in the offen," the two young people had to explain to the respective committees every alleged offense against good conduct since the days they were born. If an offense couldn't be explained satisfactorily, the culprit was made to stand up in Meeting, confess his error, and beg forgiveness.

After four or five weeks, if the investigating committees could find nothing that "might hinder proceedings," permission for the marriage was given. Then the couple would

stand up in Meeting and ask the Friends to bear witness
to the marriage. There was no further ceremony, and the
honeymoon was expected to be brief and business-like.

Friends both male and female prided themselves on
being taciturn and undemonstrative. One Quaker captain, just back from a four-year cruise, met his wife on
the sidewalk near their front door. She was carrying a
bucket en route to one of the town pumps.

"Since thee is home, thee fill it," she said, handing him
the bucket.

Another captain, about to give orders to cast off from
the dock, suddenly remembered he had forgotten to bid
his wife good-bye.

"Oh, well," he told his first mate, "after all, this time it's
a short voyage. We'll be back inside a year."

The letters exchanged by Quaker couples make fascinating reading. Whaleships in the Pacific almost always
made several stops at the Galápagos Islands, 650 miles
west of Ecuador, to capture some of the big tortoises there.
Nailed to a tree on one of the islands was a mailbox at
which outward-bound ships left mail from Nantucket and
homeward-bound vessels picked up letters from the whaling men. "Joe Doe, Ship *Bertha*, Pacific Ocean Anywhere"
was all the address that was needed on a letter from home.
One exchange of letters, over a three-year period, reads
like this:

"Dear Husband, where did thee put the cradle?"

"Dear Wife, what did thee want with the cradle?"

"Dear Husband, never mind the cradle. Where did thee
put the crib?"

Incidentally, the Galápagos turtles saved many a shipwrecked whaling man from starving to death. "Galápagos" means tortoise in Spanish, and the giant turtles on the islands weighed as much as six hundred pounds. The turtles were captured easily on the beach simply by rolling them on their backs, and they could live six months or more in the hold of a ship without food or water. Their steaks, roasted and boiled, were a welcome relief from the regular fare of long lick, a molasses drink; scouse, a stew of fat and hardtack; salt horse, dried and salted beef; and dandy funk, a dessert of powdered hardtack and molasses.

If a ship were wrecked, the survivors usually tried to take a couple of turtles along with them in the small boats.

It is difficult to say precisely why the early Nantucketers, who certainly loved liberty and admired individuality, put up with the busy-body tyranny of their church. Part of the answer may be that the Quakers considered themselves to be the Brahman class, and it was a mark of distinction to wear the drab "uniform" and use the stilted, old-fashioned language replete with "thees" and "thous."

But even more important, the Friends were basically *good* people. They didn't fine or torture offenders of their rigid code. They simply ostracized them. Viewed in terms of other punishments of the day—such as burning at the stake and cutting off hands and ears—ostracism was a mild price to pay. No one was *forced* to be a Quaker. But if a person *wanted* to be a Quaker, he had to conform. There was no persecution of Presbyterians, Baptists, or Nothingarians. The jail was usually empty, and there were few humiliating punishments such as the whipping post

and the stocks, once the Quakers gained power. The
Friends were completely honest, deplored violence, looked
after their poor, considered all men and women equal,
and practically eliminated debt, poverty, and alcoholism
on Nantucket. And they took very literally indeed the
maxim about the devil finding mischief for idle hands.

Quoting Crèvecoeur again:

"Idleness is the most heinous sin that can be committed
on Nantucket. Literally speaking, they (Nantucket men)
are never idle. Even if they go to the market place . . .
they always have a piece of cedar in their hands. And
while they are talking, they will employ themselves in
converting it into something useful."

Quakerism thrived on hardships, but it couldn't stand
prosperity. So when the Friends got rich from whale oil,
some of them wanted to build nice big houses, get a serv-
ant or two, dress their wives prettily, and stop whittling
bungs for oil casks every time they went to market. When
a select committee called on them and told them they'd
be set aside if they didn't mend their ways, some of them
decided that their wealth gave them all the prestige they
needed, and readily accepted ex-communication.

By the time of the Civil War, Quakerism was all but
dead on Nantucket. But then, so was the whaling industry, which—along with the Quakers—had enabled a barren little island to make its mark in the world.

No literature or art of any consequence stemmed from
the Quaker domination of Nantucket. But from England
to Chile to China, wherever the island's sailing ships had
ventured, a Nantucketer's word was his bond.

4. COUSIN DEB AND AUNT KEZIAH

Although the Quakers managed to keep Nantucket neutral in the Revolutionary War, twenty-one islanders served aboard John Paul Jones' privateer *Ranger*, and Jones said his crew was the "best afloat." Most of those twenty-one also volunteered to serve on Jones' next ship, the *Bon Homme Richard*, named in honor of Benjamin Franklin's *Poor Richard's Almanack*.

The *Richard* was a rotting old hulk which Jones wheedled from the French. She had been named the *Duc de Duras*, and was in the East Indian trade until she had been condemned by her owners as unfit. The American naval hero converted her into a makeshift frigate by mounting six eighteen-pounders and some other smaller guns on her decks.

Sailing out of France, he harassed British shipping quite

successfully. As a result, he had several hundred English prisoners aboard on September 23, 1779, when he sighted the brand-new British frigate *Serapis* off Flamborough Head on England's east coast. The *Serapis*, pride of the British Navy, had twenty eighteen-pounders and many smaller guns. She could fire broadsides of more than twice the weight of the *Richard's*.

Some of the French warships sailing with Jones took one look at the new, double-mounted frigate of George III and fled for the French coast. But Jones decided to engage her. The subsequent three-and-a-half-hour battle by moonlight is one of the most famous in naval history.

The very first time Jones brought his six eighteen-pounders into action, they burst and were useless for the rest of the fight. Each time the *Richard* was hit, her rotten planks gave way. But Jones ordered every prisoner to pump or drown, and kept peppering the man-of-war from his floating sieve.

The first man killed aboard the American ship was a Nantucketer, Thomas Turner. But another Nantucketer, Henry Gardner, helped save the day by leading a group of men up the *Richard's* splintered masts and lobbing hand grenades at the British cannon. The grenades didn't damage the cannon, but they demoralized the gun crews. And then one lucky throw hit a pile of ammunition, and the resulting explosion cleared a deck.

Somehow or other, Jones managed to keep his sieve afloat until the British skipper, a Captain Pearson, had had enough, and struck his colors. Jones quickly transferred all of his men and prisoners to the *Serapis*, while the *Richard* went to the bottom.

Thus the battle was won by the ship that sank. Jones was understandably proud of his crew—and the French were amazed—when he sailed the brand-new frigate back to the French port from which he had departed earlier as a comic, quixotic admiral riding the bridge of a condemned East Indiaman.

Another of Jones' boys was Reuben Chase, a strapping youth who later ran a store at the north corner of Main and Centre Streets. Chase was pictured as "Long Tom Coffin," in a poem called *The Pilot* by James Fenimore Cooper, and he had a sister named Deborah who was the island's Powerful Katrinka. Cousin Deborah Chase was just as brave as her brother, and even bigger. She weighed 350 pounds!

People in those days weren't as tactful as they are now about staring at freaks and baiting them. And occasionally sailors "from off," who didn't know about Deborah's terrific strength, would tease her when they passed her on the street.

She was a good-natured Quaker girl, and possessed considerable quiet dignity, despite her oversized appearance. Usually, she'd smile in a friendly way and otherwise ignore the teasing, as she waddled along like an overloaded frigate. But there are a couple of recorded instances when the teasing went too far.

Although Quakers didn't drink or sell liquor, there were a few grog shops on Nantucket run by non-Quakers, where a sailor could buy beer and rum. As Cousin Deborah passed by a grog shop one afternoon, someone inside gave a whoop and a dozen sailors "from off" came pouring out on the sidewalk to have a better look at her.

They guffawed and pointed, but the fat girl merely shrugged and looked straight ahead, minding her manners even if they didn't know how to mind theirs.

Then one of the sailors, pretty thoroughly in his cups, decided to yield to an overwhelming temptation to pinch her oscillating and more than ample stern.

Falling in behind her and doing his best to imitate her walk, he crept up with a thumb and forefinger extended, while his comrades roared encouragement.

Deborah might ignore gibes and drunken laughter, but no Quaker girl could possibly allow her stern to be pinched under any circumstances. And the thought that this drunken oaf intended not only to pinch her stern but to pinch it in front of an audience was more than Deborah could bear.

Suddenly, as if she had eyes in the back of her head, she pirouetted as lightly as a dancer and cuffed his extended arm so hard that he spun half-way around. Then she grabbed him by the nape of his neck and the seat of his pants, and threw him into the air. The startled sailor executed a half somersault and landed head first on the roof of a one-story shanty. Without a glance at the others in his now silent group, Deb proceeded to waddle on her way. Needless to say, none of the other sailors volunteered to follow her with outstretched fingers.

Mr. F. C. Sanford, a Nantucketer who knew Reuben Chase and his sister, wrote some recollections about them. Sanford said that the man thrown onto the roof by the powerful Deborah was "of 160 pounds weight."

In 1777 British forces raided the island, posted sentries around town, and ordered everyone to stay indoors. Deborah obeyed the order for awhile. But when her family needed water, she decided to make a trip to the nearest public pump.

Although her father implored her not to leave the house, she assured him she would be all right. Taking two pails, she waddled out the front door and down the street toward the pump. As she reached the corner, a rough sentry poked a bayonet in the general direction of her bulging stomach and remarked none too civilly:

"All right, Fat Girl, where do you think you're going?"

"None of thy business," responded the Fat Girl.

"Get back in your house before I drag you down to the try works and boil you down for oil," the sentry smirked. "My orders are . . ."

There was a resounding "bong!" as Cousin Deb—who could stand almost anything except being compared with a whale—swung a bucket in a full circle and brought it down on the sentry's head. Then she proceeded to the pump, got her water, and started home. The sentry was still fast asleep on the sidewalk, as the Fat Girl picked up her skirts and stepped over him.

Deborah's most famous feat of strength, though, climaxed a lengthy feud with a drayman almost as strong as herself. This individual carted hogsheads from a cooper's shop to the wharfs. The Chases' house was on a corner along his route, and like most Nantucket houses it stood almost on the street. The big drayman, sitting atop his hogsheads, would cut the corner so sharply with his four galloping horses that the wagon often brushed against the Chases' residence, with a fearful clatter.

The noise began to get on the nerves of all the Chases,

even the nerves of normally phlegmatic Deborah. But when she sought out the drayman and asked him to swing wider around the corner, he paid no attention. Indeed, he seemed to make a point, thereafter, to be sure to hit the house. And when Deborah came running to the window to remonstrate with him, he'd holler, "Thar she blows," over his shoulder, while his dray careened down the street.

As previously noted, Cousin Deb did not appreciate any comparison, however subtle, between herself and a whale. So after three or four days of the "Thar she blows" treatment, she was waiting for him on the corner when he came roaring up, and brushed the house again with his cart, as usual. Seeing her, he grinned, waved his hat, and shouted at the top of his voice, "Thar she blows, she blows, she . . ."

But at that point Deb stepped to the side of the wagon and gave it a mighty heave. Over went the driver, the hogsheads, and the dray, in a terrible mess. The horses came loose from the wagon, whinnied hellishly, and dashed off down the street with the rolling hogsheads hot on their heels. When the horses had disappeared and the hogsheads had stopped rolling, Deborah addressed the conscious but recumbent figure of the big drayman.

"Thee must learn to drive more carefully and thee must learn not to refer to ladies as whales," she admonished him, not ungently.

They say the drayman needed the help of nine other men to turn the wagon back on its wheels.

Another Nantucketer who didn't like to be stared at was a hunchback whose name I haven't been able to find out.

I *do* know, though, that he was a sailor, and that he was aboard the ship *Bedford* when she anchored just below the Tower of London, in the Thames, February 3, 1783.

The *Bedford,* commanded by Captain William Mooers and bringing a cargo of whale oil from Nantucket, caused a furor by hoisting the Stars and Stripes. It was the first time that the new American flag had been flown in any British port—Cornwallis had surrendered, but no formal peace treaty had been signed. Naturally, the Americans didn't get a very cordial reception when they went cockily ashore.

One British sailor came up to the Nantucket hunchback, squeezed the lump on his back, and hollered insultingly:

"Ho there, my Little Dwarf, what are you hiding under your jacket?"

"Bunker Hill, and be damned to thee," replied the hunchback, swinging a roundhouse uppercut which decked his tormentor.

The *Bedford* had cleared from the Rotch—pronounced Roach—Market, a brick building which is still a familiar landmark at the foot, or harbor end, of Nantucket's wide, cobblestoned Main Street. William Rotch was one of the leading mrechants and factors in the American colonies, and he built his market as his office and counting house in 1774. After the Revolution, it also doubled as an American Custom House. Fifty years ago, the Rotch Market was a clubhouse for retired Nantucket captains, who played checkers and cribbage there, and swapped lies. Today, all the retired captains except some self-appointed ones are dead. But the market, now the Pacific Club, is still a gathering place for old men who play checkers and cribbage, and swap lies.

Painted on the outside walls of the Pacific Club are the names of the ships *Dartmouth, Eleanor,* and *Beaver.* These vessels, owned by William Rotch and his brother, sailed from Nantucket in 1772 with whaleoil for the lamps of London. The ships were chartered in London by the East India Company, and sent back to Boston with a cargo of tea for the colonists. While in Boston harbor, the three vessels were boarded by "Indians" who tossed the cargo over the side, in the famous Boston Tea Party. Because Rotch was a good friend of John Hancock's, the ships weren't damaged by the "Indians."

Another Nantucket captain, Shubael Coffin, was the master of Hancock's brig *Harrison,* and brought to Boston the first news of the repeal of the Stamp Act.

Rotch was among those Quakers who managed to keep Nantucket neutral. Exposed as it was to British men-of-war, the island could not be protected by the Colonists. And it wasn't worth protecting by the British. So it would have been suicide for Nantucketers to declare their allegiance to either side. Also, Nantucketers knew that if they were blockaded for long by either side, they would starve and freeze.

In spite of its neutrality, Nantucket suffered unbelievable hardships during both the Revolution and the War of 1812. There was never enough food or fuel. In violation of treaties, the English captured Nantucket ships, impressed Nantucket seamen, and at intervals blockaded the island.

Both the British and the Americans continually accused Nantucketers of "dealing with the enemy." In disciplinary

actions for alleged infractions of neutrality, American provincial troops raided the island in 1775 and confiscated
flour which they said was consigned to the British. And
British raiders sailed into the harbor in eight ships April
6, 1779, and seized property valued at $50,000. Some Nan-
tucket houses built during that period have secret rooms
and passages—usually camouflaged around chimneys
which are not quite as wide as they look—in which "trai-
tors" and articles of value were hidden from the raiders.

Incredible as it seems, neutral Nantucket with a population of slightly more than 4,500 lost 1,600 lives and 134
ships between 1775 and 1781. Of course, if Nantucket
hadn't been neutral, it almost certainly would have been
wiped out altogether by one side or the other.

Among those Nantucketers who didn't grow cold or
hungry during the Revolution was Mrs. Keziah Folger
Coffin. At one time she was "Dear Cousin Keziah" to her
off-island kinsman, Benjamin Franklin. But that was before Keziah started smuggling, trading with the British,
and profiteering. It's doubtful if Franklin would have
"cousined" her after that.

Since almost all Nantucketers were close relatives, virtually all adults were known by their given names—with
an "Aunt," "Uncle," or "Cousin" prefixed. The lady profi-
teer was universally known as "Aunt Keziah."

She was an angular, shrewd, insensitive woman, with
a heart full of courage and meanness. She loved money and
she especially loved outsharping someone in a business
transaction. Few deals were deemed too large, too small,
or too sneaky for Aunt Keziah.

So she played the British Crown against the Continental

Congress, and cheated the socks off both of them. But even while she was doing this, and raking in thousands of dollars and pounds, she seemed to get almost equal enjoyment out of taking candy from children, by short-changing them when they traded at a little store she ran in her home.

Keziah's husband, Jethro Coffin, was a whaling man. When he went to sea shortly after their wedding, he left his young wife in extremely modest circumstances. But when he came home again just before the Revolutionary War, she was rolling delightfully in wealth. In fact she was the richest person—man or woman—on Nantucket. Also, for flaunting her wealth and wearing gaily colored London clothes, she had been "set aside" by the Friends —but she couldn't have cared less.

Jethro, bewildered but not unhappy about his sudden affluence, attempted to question Keziah about the source of the money. But she kissed him in un-Quaker fashion and promised him that if he asked her no questions, she'd tell him no lies.

The fact was that, while Jethro was at sea, Keziah's little shop had started featuring such items as crimson shawls for ladies; good, English woolens; hard-to-get tea; a spinet piano.

Of course the town buzzed with gossip about where she got the items. Everyone knew that Aunt Keziah had recently bought a house out at Quaise, an isolated section of the inner harbor. There were reports that large rowboats with muffled oars sometimes landed on the beach in front of the house, at night. Some people said there was a tunnel that ran from the beach to the basement. At any rate, everyone knew that Aunt Keziah was cheating the Crown out of customs duties, by handling smuggled goods.

But when the British started blockading the Atlantic Coast, Keziah's smuggled goods couldn't come through. Immediately declaring herself a full-fledged Tory, she wrote heart-rending letters to George III and to the British Admiral Digby, in command of the blockade squadron in New York.

Her letters said quite correctly that the people of Nantucket had to have food or they would starve; less correctly that Nantucket was unanimously Tory; and entirely incorrectly that she had always stood ready to dedicate her worldly goods, her life, and her sacred honor to England.

Touched by this expression of devotion, His Majesty and His Majesty's Admiral allowed Keziah's ships—but no one else's—to pass through the blockade. And while Nantucketers were starving, their "Aunt's" storehouses were bulging with food.

She built a new store and an elaborate house in Centre Street—by far the most expensive house in town. And she sold sugar for $3.50 a cup and tea for $9 a pound!

Crèvecoeur, the writer, met Aunt Keziah and her husband while they were riding high. But apparently he missed the point as to how she had obtained her wealth. At any rate, he recorded:

"The richest person on the island owes all of his present prosperity and success to the ingenuity of his wife . . . While he was performing his first cruises, she traded with pins and needles . . . Afterwards, she purchased more considerable articles . . . She wrote to London and formed connections . . . Who of Nantucket or Boston does not know of Aunt Keziah? I must tell you that she is the wife of Mr. C——n, a very respectable man."

Most Nantucketers couldn't meet Keziah's scandalous prices. When they pointed out to her that they had to eat, she graciously consented to take mortgages on their homes and businesses. In short, she became the island's foremost skinflint, and of course that entitled her automatically to serious consideration as world's champion in that category.

At about the mid-point of the Revolution, she was charged with treason to the new Republic, and went personally to Boston to clear herself. Acting as her own attorney and denying with injured feelings that she was a Tory, she over-awed the court and was acquitted.

Her comeuppance came, however, when Nantucket convinced the Crown that it was trying to be neutral, and the Crown lifted the blockade. That broke Aunt Keziah's monopoly, and prices tumbled.

Her warehouses, still jammed with goods she had bought on credit at war-risk prices, now stood idle. When she tried to sell these goods to pay off her notes, no one would buy. In desperation, she put on the market various pieces of property she had obtained by foreclosure. But the islanders wouldn't bid against each other. Usually there was only one bid—and it was extremely low—by the person who had lost the property. So Aunt Keziah's financial empire collapsed.

Muttering darkly about the ingratitude of people who had turned against her after she had fed them in their hour of need, Aunt Keziah left the island in a huff and vowed she would never return. But some years later, in 1790, she changed her mind and *did* return—and she was just as ornery, unrepentant, and fiercely brave as in the days when she owned half the town and was foreclosing mortgages and evicting her widowed kinfolk, right and left.

The first thing she did on reaching the island was to hire a local lawyer and instruct him to go to court and get back all her property. He told her she didn't have a chance of winning. But perhaps Aunt Keziah had been motivated, right from the beginning, not so much by the desire to accumulate vast wealth as by the enjoyment of occupying the center of the ring in a grandstand fight— one lone, unconventional, defiant woman against the combined smug forces of the whole community.

"I want thee to keep this case in court as long as I live," she told her lawyer.

As it turned out, that wasn't very long. A few days later, as she was hurrying down a flight of steps to go to court and listen to the lawyer present her case, she tripped and broke her neck.

In a few minutes she was dead. There were a few uncharitable souls on the island who whispered that she had done herself a job that the hangman should have done fifteen years before.

5. "TRYING OUT" WHALES

A school of miniature whales was sighted during the summer of 1918 off the Nantucket harbor jetties, directly in front of our cottage and two lighthouses. The animals were small killer whales of the genus globicphalus, commonly called blackfish—although whales are not fish but mammals. They were ten to sixteen feet long, and their presence off an old whaling town caused a great deal of excitement.

A couple of young Nantucketers, perhaps descendants of the brave whalers of yore, chugged out to the end of the jetties in small fishing boats and started to herd the blackfish.

My father, watching the herding through binoculars from an open window at the top of his three-story lighthouse, shouted down to us a detailed running account.

Dad enjoyed nothing more than an interested audience and the center of the stage. So it was perhaps inevitable that within a matter of minutes he was playing to the hilt the role of lookout in the crows-nest of a pitching whaleship.

"Thar she blows," he called, holding the binoculars with one hand and the to'gallant cross-tree—or at any rate the windowsill—with the other, while he swayed from side to side. "She"—Dad's head disappeared for a minute, as he pretended to have lost his footing; but in a moment he was back again, still gamely clutching the binoculars—"blows."

I suppose that blackfish really do blow, but their geysers must be mighty puny. If you could believe Dad's account, they were blowing by the score. "Blows, blows, blows," he bellowed. "Two points off the larboard bow and she blows."

"Can I come up and look through the binoculars, Daddy?" I shouted up to him.

"Blows," said Dad.

"Can I, Daddy?" I insisted.

"Me, too," yelled three or four of my brothers and sisters, employing an expression which gets quite a bit of use in a large family.

"There's only room in the crows-nest for one," sang out Dad. "Blows, blows."

There was certainly room at the top of Dad's lighthouse for more than one. But I knew there wasn't room for all of us, and that he wouldn't play favorites or take time out, as he sometimes did, to let us draw lots. So I didn't press the point.

Suddenly forgetting that he was the lookout, Dad

stopped swaying and even let loose his grip on the "cross-tree."

"The idiots!" he hollered. "What do those idiots in the motorboats want to bring the whales in *here* for? I thought they were trying to drive them out to sea. But, by jingo, the idiots are driving them ashore."

"Is she blowing, Daddy?" one of my young brothers inquired. "Blows, blows, blows, Daddy?"

But Dad was all through playing whaleman.

"Do you know that those idiots are doing?" he said, more to himself than for our benefit. "They're not only herding those blackfish ashore, they're heading them right for *my bathing beach*."

We thought this was splendid news indeed, since it would give us a chance to see the blackfish close up. But our lookout, still peering through the binoculars and so excited that we were afraid he might *really* tumble out of the window, was simply furious. It was difficult to tell whether Dad was more upset about the possible needless slaughter of the blackfish or the effrontery of trespass on "his" bathing beach. Actually, the beach belonged to the town, but Dad used it.

"Why do you want to kill those beautiful fish?" he demanded, as if the men in the motorboats could hear him. "They're no good to eat. If you want to play at killing whales, why don't you pick on a full-grown whale? And I'll tell you one thing, if you drive so much as one blackfish onto my bathing beach you'll be sorry. Yes sir, you'll rue the day."

"Does she blow, blow, blow, Daddy?" the young brother called up insistently.

But now that the blackfish were about to be killed, Dad refused to think of them as whales—even as miniature whales.

"Those little fellows can't really blow," he explained. "Why the old-time Nantucketers wouldn't even have used those little fellows for bait. But I'll guarantee you this: If those men drive those fish onto my bathing beach . . . Come on, let's go down there and get a look."

Dad descended, and emerged from his lighthouse. Absently, in an action which he had repeated countless times during the last ten years, he looked for the smallest child, found him, and hoisted him onto his shoulders. Then he led the way to "his" beach, which was about three hundred yards from our house and immediately adjacent to the Cliff Beach Bathhouse, where most of the summer people swam.

By the time we arrived at the water, it was apparent that the blackfish would be stranded not only on "Dad's" beach but on the Cliff Beach as well. In fact there were so many of the torpedo-shaped little whales, each one about the size of a rowboat, that they weren't going to leave any room at all to swim near the jetties.

The blackfish came into shallow water and went aground. You could hear them panting—that's right, *panting;* and it gives you the creeps to hear a "fish" breathe— as they struggled unsuccessfully to get free. Dad's anger at having trespassers on his beach had long since turned to silent disgust. Five or six men bearing weapons ranging from old whaling spears to Civil War swords leaped barefoot from stranded fish to stranded fish, in a gruesome slaughter of gushing blood. I guess they were afraid that when the tide came in, the blackfish might swim away. The water turned red for a half-mile or so along the shore. That isn't a figure of speech. It was real red, and frothy. I'll never forget it. After awhile, you could hear only three or four blackfish panting, and then none at all. And the low waves which washed up in the beach turned the sand a dirty pinkish color.

Dad let us watch it all, and I have never seen him more thoroughly revolted.

"It isn't nice to see," he told us, "but you mustn't let things like that make you sick. I wanted you to watch it, and now I want you to remember it. I don't like people who kill things for no reason at all. And I don't want you to like them, either."

"Particularly when they kill things on your bathing beach, eh Daddy?" someone asked him. "Who wants to go swimming in red water with a lot of dead whales that might all of a sudden come to life again, eh Daddy?"

"Particularly then," Dad nodded absently. "Come on, let's get out of here."

We went back to our cottage. But having a whole school of miniature whales right in our front yard, so to speak, offered Dad an opportunity—much too good to be overlooked—to give us a few lessons in natural science. He drove down to the Atheneum library, got out a couple of books on whales, and did a little quick homework.

"I was wrong about blackfish not being good to eat," he told us later that afternoon. "The books say they're delicious. There's a diagram here that shows the best parts to eat. I'm going down and get us a few blackfish steaks."

That's just what he did, too. Carrying a long carving knife, a big fork, some old newspapers, and the book with the diagram, he walked back to the beach—with the smallest child on his shoulders, of course. The rest of us tagged along. Placing the book on top of one of the little whales, and propping the leaves open with a couple of pebbles, he attacked the cadaver skillfully.

Dad came from a generation in which men carried knives from the day they were old enough to have pockets. The carving knife was sharp, and the steaks were cut cleanly and evenly. We watched fascinated—and so did a couple of thousand other people who had converged on the beach to see the corpses.

"May I ask," one gentleman in the audience inquired politely of Dad, "what you intend to do with that whale-meat?"

"Eat it," said Dad, intent on his work.

"You wouldn't be going to all that trouble just to throw those good steaks away, would you Daddy?" one of my young brothers commented.

"Sure wouldn't," Dad conceded.

"Are you going to feed it to your children, too?" asked the gentleman.

"I think so," Dad nodded. "I'll try it first myself."

"Is it good to eat?"

"This book says it is," said Dad.

The word spread quickly if prematurely not only that blackfish meat was good to eat but that the Gilbreths—the family in the lighthouses with all the red-haired children—had eaten it without bad effects even to the baby.

Summer visitors to Nantucket in those days were generally well-to-do. But the lure of something-for-nothing has a universal appeal. When we had arrived at the beach, not a single blackfish had been mutilated. But by the time Dad had finished carving, and was wrapping the steaks in the newspapers, several hundred well-dressed people with carving knives had arrived on the scene, to swell the original crowd of some two thousand. And then some of the two thousand started heading for home to get knives too.

The mass assault on the corpses—there were 128 of them by actual count—left intestines and other entrails too numerous and revolting to mention scattered all the way from the high-water mark to the bathhouse. Did you know that a full-grown blue whale has two and a half miles of intestines? Dad's book said so, and I am prepared to believe it right down to the last half inch.

Blackfish, if not exactly as delicious as Dad alleged, at any rate certainly is edible. In the interest of economy, we ate it until it came out our ears. So did a good many other people on the island. Even the local hotels featured blackfish fillets on their menus.

And then the weather turned warm, flies assembled from distant points, and the whole island had a horrid, fishy smell. Around our house, which was nearer to the beach than any other human habitation, the smell was enough to keep you awake nights. The hotels stopped featuring blackfish on their menu, and Dad found pressing business to attend to back in New York. "No one is ever going to convince me that ambergris or anything else from one of these creatures has any place in perfume," Dad remarked, with his handkerchief in front of his nose, shortly before boarding the steamer for the mainland.

Of course no one would go near the beach, let alone go swimming. The business of the Cliff Beach Bathhouse was ruined, and the whole summer tourist trade was threatened. So finally the city fathers hired someone with a strong stomach and an insensitive nose to tie the mutilated corpses together and tow them out to sea, where they were cut loose. Even so, from time to time for the rest of the summer, the noisome cadavers would return by twos and threes and wash ashore. Needless to say, by then they were somewhat past the stage of being overripe, and they invariably caused consternation.

I am told now that the reason the blackfish were harpooned in the first place was that someone intended to "try them out," which is to say to fry their blubber for oil. Even today, a single big sperm whale may be worth five thousand dollars to its slaughterers because there is still a good market for whale oil. It is used as a high-grade lubricant, and also in the manufacture of some of the best cold creams, paints, textiles, and soaps.

A useful little book called the *Nantucket Argument Settlers* advances the theory that the purpose of the mass slaughter was to get oil. It says, under the heading of August 3, 1918:

"Another school of blackfish stranded on Cliff Bathing Beach. One hundred and twenty-eight were killed. No way to try out oil, and carcasses were finally towed out to sea and set adrift. Many persons indulged in blackfish steak, which was served in some of the hotels."

That item implies that the fish stranded themselves, instead of being driven ashore. Perhaps that's what really happened. But there *were* motorboats around them, because I saw them and so did a certain lookout who had a perfect view through binoculars from the top of his private lighthouse.

I guess it would be unwise to get into an argument with the *Argument Settlers,* because the very name of that praiseworthy volume indicates I would be merely wasting my breath and re-hashing something that had long since been gone into thoroughly, weighed from every angle, and decided with finality.

I *do* think, though, that if I had been writing the item I could have found a better verb than "indulge," to describe what many persons did with the blackfish steaks. "Indulge" means—at any rate connotes—the gluttonous yielding to an insatiable temptation. Anyone who sampled blackfish steak, and still was insatiably tempted to make a pig of himself for reasons other than economy, should have his head examined, let alone his bloated stomach.

Also, I think the item would have been more complete if *Argument Settlers* had given credit where credit is due. The book could well have recorded the name of the summer visitor who, on the say-so of a library book, carved the first steak from one of the 128 corpses, and then joined his wife and children in "trying it out." I trust that my account here will amplify the record.

I have done considerable reading about whales since that time. While I am no expert, there is one aspect of whaling on which I doff my cap to no living man. The whaling books, both old and new, go into great detail to describe just how unspeakably terrible the whaling vessels smelled, especially in equatorial waters and after dismembered pieces of the leviathans had been stored on deck pending their "trying." In fact, merchant sailors used to remark distastefully that they could "smell a whaleship twenty miles to leeward." But the books don't have to tell *me* how a whaleship used to smell. I *know*.

6. WHEN WHALE WAS KING

Whale was king on Nantucket for the better part of two centuries. More than fifty years before Paul Revere's ride, Nantucketers were sailing all the way up to the Arctic Circle in search of whales. Shortly after the Revolutionary War, the Quaker sea captains were doubling the Horn, pursuing their prey into the uncharted vastness of the Pacific.

Whaling involved more discomforts and called for more daring than any other adventurous job—short of war and piracy—the world has ever known.

Nantucket Quakers, who were conscientious objectors to war, were the best whalers on earth.

Nantucketers sailed their tubby, bluff-bowed little ships to any place on the globe where they suspected there might be whales. Their prey was the biggest animal on earth, and their weapons were as primitive as those of Caesar's soldiers. For continuous stretches of three or four years at a time, the ocean was their home. Typhoons, cannibals, British and Spanish men-of-war, hidden coral reefs, and pirates all took their toll of Nantucketers. But nothing could stop them from coming back to waters where the whales were.

And so the Nantucketers, with their square-toed shoes and Quaker homespun, knew the streets of London, Madrid, Valparaiso, and Singapore. But many of them didn't know a thing about Boston, Philadelphia, or New York—and some of them had never even been to the mainland of their own country.

"Two-thirds of this terraqueous globe are the Nantucketer's" Melville wrote in his classic description in *Moby Dick*. "For the sea is his; he owns it as emperors own empires, other seamen having but a right-of-way through it. Merchant ships are but extension bridges . . . The Nantucketer, he alone resides and riots on the sea; he alone, in Bible language, goes down to it in ships; to and fro plowing it as his own special plantation. *There* is his home; *there* lies his business."

The whale is not only the biggest animal now on earth, but the biggest animal that has *ever* been on earth. Compared with a whale, even the biggest dinosaurs were puny.

Whales have been killed which were 111 feet long and weighed ninety tons—bigger than a thousand men—and there probably were even bigger whales which got away. Some whales can open their jaws thirty feet wide. They have a mouth bigger than the average living room. Their tongue weighs as much as an entire elephant, and a male whale's sex organ is ten feet long.

No one seems to be sure, but whales apparently live for fifty years, and possibly considerably longer. They are true mammals—have warm blood, breathe air, and would drown if they stayed under water too long. Some species can hold their breath for at least fifty minutes and some can dive a mile deep, where the pressures would make jelly of a man. When whales emerge from a dive, they exhale a cloud of watery vapor from a blowhole or blow-holes (the sperm whale has one; the blue whale two) at the top of the head. This cloud rises, geyser fashion, as high as fifty feet into the air, and is the "blow" that mast-head lookouts watch for.

Some whales, the blues for example, are monogamous. But the prized cachalots or sperms travel around in harems, with a bull in charge. When another cachalot bull shows up, the two males back away and then rush forward at speeds of thirty to thirty-five miles an hour, to butt heads with a sickening impact. Imagine three locomotives in tandem having a head-on collision with three other locomotives in tandem, and perhaps you'll get the picture. The bulls also bite bungalow-sized chunks out of each other, and swat back and forth with tails powerful enough to cave in the side of a wooden ship. The loser finally slinks away, presumably with a whale of a headache.

Georges Blond, the French authority and author of *The Great Story of Whales,* says that whales make love just as all other warm-blooded mammals, and that during the mating season that's all the males think about. M. Blond made a pretty thorough study of the matter. He reports that the bull and cow gambol and caress each other, and that the bull capers, shows off, nips the cow playfully, and gives her clumsy love pats with flippers that can be heard two miles away.

The whale calf is born in about a year, and may be twenty-five feet long and weigh ten tons. There have been a few cases of twins. The female suckles her calf, and the milk looks exactly like cow's milk. M. Blond says a baby blue whale gains about ten pounds an hour.

The killer whales are the smartest species. Some mariners believe the killers are the most intelligent animals alive—second only to man. They sometimes hunt in wolf packs, and thus are able to slay even the gigantic blue whales. A killer has been known to surface near a block of ice on which a seal was safely floating; to survey the situation with malevolent eye; and then to submerge, come up under the block of ice, and see-saw it until the terrified seal fell off.

Scientists are pretty well agreed that all whales once lived on land and walked on four legs. The front legs now are flippers, and traces of the back legs can be found in the skeleton structure.

Nantucketers went after the biggest of whales, in open boats smaller than the mouth of their prey. Arm a mouse with a pin, put him in a toy automobile, and send him out to attack an elephant—and you'll have a comparable situation in regard to size.

The first whaling at Nantucket was of the "off-shore" variety. When lookouts along the beach saw a whale, they signaled boat crews which rowed out and attacked the animal. Then his carcass was towed ashore and his blubber tried out. Nantucketers killed their first whale in this manner in 1672. Meanwhile, the same thing was going on at Cape Cod, and in 1690 the Nantucketers hired a "Capie," Ichabod Paddock, to come to the island and teach them everything he knew.

Small sail boats soon supplemented the rowboats in chasing down the whales sighted from shore. Then in 1712, a small whaling sloop belonging to Christopher Hussey was blown out to sea in a gale. After the wind died down and Hussey was headed back to Nantucket, he sighted a whole school of spermaceti whales. He managed to kill one and to tow parts of it back to the island. And thus the business of hunting the oceans for whales was born.

The "sperm" whale was much more valuable than the "right" whales which Nantucketers had caught off shore. In addition to its blubber, the sperm has a cavity in the top of its head containing a ton of the highest-grade oil. You could climb into the head cavity and bail out the contents with a bucket.

By 1732, little Nantucket sloops of forty tons were hunting whales as far north as the Davis Straits between Greenland and Baffin Island. And when a Captain Atkins brought home a live Greenland bear that year, it caused a national sensation.

In 1759, the first square-rigged whaling ship was fitted out on Nantucket. This was the fore-runner of a whole fleet of three-masters seaworthy enough to go anywhere.

They had cranes to hoist aboard segments of whales, brick tryworks to boil down the blubber, and hundreds of hogsheads to store the oil.

It was with these ships that Nantucketers plowed the oceans as they had never been plowed before. Explorers had preceded the Nantucketers, of course, and merchantmen were sailing in as straight a line as possible between various ports. But the Nantucketers began to cross and recross almost every mile of ocean, discovering new islands, mapping shoals, learning about weather and currents.

It is impossible to overemphasize the importance of all this, on the history of the world. For instance, when Captain Timothy Folger figured out the workings of the Gulf Stream, he sketched a rough map and sent it to his Philadelphia kinsman, Benjamin Franklin. Franklin had the map engraved for him, and it revolutionized commerce between Europe and America. Franklin's mother, as already mentioned, was a Nantucket Folger, and Franklin himself missed being born on Nantucket by only two months. The Folgers had a scientific bent, and were known on the island as being "facultized."

The first Nantucket whaleship to double Cape Horn was the *Beaver,* captained by Paul Worth, which made the dangerous journey in 1791. Thereafter, Nantucketers began to cross-plow the Pacific as they had the Atlantic. The Pacific was almost completely unknown at that time, and the world was still goggle-eyed at the stories of Captain James Cook's re-discovery of Hawaii—then known as the Sandwich Islands. Only thirteen years before Worth's voyage, Cook, the English explorer, had landed at Hawaii, where the

Polynesians first had fallen to the ground and worshiped him as Lono, god of harvest, and then had murdered him in revenge for a flogging administered to a native who stole a boat.

The whalers themselves discovered hundreds of islands in the Pacific where the natives had never seen white men before. More than thirty Pacific islands and reefs are named for Nantucketers.

One of the most surprising "finds" of Nantucketers in the Pacific, although not exactly a discovery, occurred February 6, 1808. On that date, Captain Mayhew Folger sailed the *Topaz* up to the supposedly uninhabited island of Pitcairn, to replenish his supply of fresh water. He was amazed to see a group of handsome boys put out from Pitcairn in a canoe, and approach the *Topaz*. And when the boys hailed the *Topaz* in English, with a Cockney accent, Folger was speechless.

Inadvertently, Folger had blundered upon the hiding place of the mutineers of Captain William Bligh's armed transport, HMS *Bounty*—and thus had solved one of the most intriguing maritime mysteries of all time.

Captain Folger and his crew went ashore and received a warm welcome from the last of the mutineers, a white-haired old Englishman named Alexander Smith. Smith was the unofficial king of the island, presiding benevolently over a small group of middle-aged but still handsome Polynesian women and twenty or more "beautiful children."

The mutiny on the *Bounty* occurred in 1789, when Fletcher Christian and his bully-boys seized command and cast adrift Captain Bligh and eighteen loyal members of the crew. The mutineers then sailed the *Bounty* to Tahiti, where some of them elected to remain, and eventually were captured, taken to England, and hanged on Execution Dock. But Christian and eight other mutineers, along with twelve Tahitian women and six Tahitian menservants, sailed to uninhabited Pitcairn. There they burned the *Bounty*, so that her hulk wouldn't attract searchers to their hiding place.

For nineteen years, the British Navy had been looking for the mutineers, to bring them to justice. During that time, all of the culprits had died except Alexander Smith. At Folger's suggestion, Smith changed his named to John Adams, to confuse the British admiralty.

Smith gave Folger the chronometer from the *Bounty*. When the *Topaz* reached civilization with proof that the mystery had been solved, Folger's news threw the maritime world into an uproar.

I don't see how Smith's changing his name to Adams could have been very confusing to the British admiralty, particularly after Folger told the whole story of his adventure. But for some reason, the admiralty decided to allow Smith—or Adams—to remain unmolested with his harem in the middle of the Pacific, where he died in 1829.

There are scores of hard-to-believe but well documented coincidences about whaling. For instance, Captain Peter Paddok of the *Lady Adams* killed a whale in 1815, and when the animal was butchered it was found to contain a harpoon which Paddok had sunk into a whale thirteen years before, when he was on the ship *Lion*.

Then there's the story of First Mate Marshall Jenkins who was in charge of a boat which harpooned a sperm whale. The wounded whale pulled free, turned on the boat and bit it in two. As Jenkins fell over the side, the whale seized him in its jaws, and sounded. The rest of the men climbed into the two halves of the separated boat. The men in the forepart of the boat were talking about how it was too bad what happened to Mate Jenkins when the whale breached right next to them and spat out Jenkins at their feet. This ship's log reports that the First Mate was "much bruised," but that he recovered within a fortnight.

Merchant seamen scornfully referred to whaling vessels as "spouters," "butcher shops adrift" and "hell ships." Certainly there were times when whaleships—with their try-pots belching flames and sizzling from the fat that had been fed them—resembled floating hells. A whaleship, besides being one of the most seaworthy craft ever devised for its size, also was a combination slaughter house and oil factory. After a whale had been killed, the decks ran with blood as sweaty, half-naked men hacked the gigantic corpse to pieces, and tossed the chunks of blubber into the evil-smelling pots.

For the men before the mast, whaling meant dangerous work, impossible food, back-breaking hours, no guarantee of steady pay, and ironhanded rule from which there was no appeal. A captain could flog a man to death, or maroon him on a desert island, or keep him on bread and water until he was a skeleton.

Even after pressure was put on the merchant marine to improve the terrible conditions of common seamen, the whalemen got little consideration. As a result, it became increasingly difficult to sign on whaling crews. During the last years of large-scale whaling, the crews were composed mostly of Nantucket boys who were being trained to become mates and captains, and Negroes and foreigners who had little hope of advancement.

But regardless of maggoty food, the unbelievable stench, and working conditions a good deal worse than slavery, whaling had some compensations that the merchant service could never match.

Perhaps the biggest compensation was the thrill of the chase—the exciting job of rowing an open boat up to the biggest creature on earth, hurling a harpoon into him, and being towed by the beast on a wild "Nantucket sleighride." Whalemen used to tell their girls back home that if a man so much as shifted a cud of tobacco during a "sleighride," the boat would capsize.

There was also, of course, the possibility of "greasy luck." Each man aboard a whaleship, from the captain to the cabin boy, was entitled to a share, or "lay," of the profits of the voyage. The captain's share might be one-sixteenth and the cabin boy's one-two hundredth. Greasy luck actually did occur fairly often. For instance, the *Sarah* returned to Nantucket in 1830 after a three-year voyage with $98,000 worth of "ile." The *Loper,* in the shortest successful voyage to the Pacific, made $50,000 in only fourteen months. The *Watchman,* in addition to "ile" and whalebone, found eight hundred pounds of ambergris in 1858, worth $10,000.

And perhaps the biggest compensation of all—for men and boys who liked excitement—was the virtual certainty of finding adventure exploring the Pacific Islands.

There was even a chance—as many a whaling skipper

reminded young men who were undecided about whether to sign on for a cruise—of finding adventure and luck right near home. For instance, there was a standing reward from 1817 through 1820 of $5,000 to any whaleship which would rid Gloucester (Massachusetts) Bay of its "100-foot sea-serpent." The serpent had eyes "as large as pewter plates," was the color of an eel, and had a long neck which protruded from the water and swayed pendulum-fashion when the hellish monster swam.

The serpent—or whatever it was—was first sighted in August 1817 by the captain of a coastal vessel. Subsequently it was seen by close to a thousand people—including a crowd of several hundred at Nahant beach, a marksman who fired a gun at the creature from a distance of less than thirty yards, and a minister-mathematician who used navigational instruments to measure the "serpent" accurately down to the last half-inch.

Many whaling ships combed Gloucester Bay for the monster during the three years that the reward was offered. Although no one caught the serpent, its "existence" so close to Nantucket gave skippers an opportunity to train their crews to keep a sharp lookout, as whaling vessels left the island and headed out to sea.

On Nantucket, whaling was the test of manhood. The more a boy heard about the discomforts and dangers, the more he wanted to demonstrate that he could face them without flinching. And the test was all the more important since some girls on the island scornfully told their land-lubber suitors that they'd never marry a man who hadn't killed a whale.

So the boys left home when they were still beardless,

half-grown, and soprano-voiced. When they returned perhaps three or four years later, they were husky men with a pocketful of money, and they were welcomed by the townspeople in the same way that other towns welcome war heroes.

"Butcher shops adrift?" That was certainly one way of looking at whaling. True enough, the whalemen didn't wear crimson scarfs around their waists or embroidered jackets and tight-fitting trousers. They didn't talk about the "moment of truth," and there were no worshiping thousands to cheer them on at the time of danger. But to the Nantucket girls, the whalemen were the matadors of the deep. And one does not call a matador a butcher—at least to his face.

So whaling had its compensations, but even at best it was a dog-eat-dog activity. At worst it was man-eat-man. Probably more than a hundred Nantucketers were eaten by cannibals. And occasionally—very occasionally—Nantucketers ate Nantucketers.

7. *ESSEX* AND THE WHALE

Nantucket's movie house, a short block from the Atheneum library and another short block from the harbor's edge, is an ungainly wooden structure named the Dreamland Theater. Back in the days of silent films, the piano accompaniment was played by a blind man. He had a young assistant who sat next to him and told him in a stage-whisper what was happening on the screen, so the music would fit the mood.

If you happened to be unlucky enough to have a front seat at the Dreamland, you couldn't help but hear the boy's graphic account.

"Now this guy with the moustache," he'd say, "grabs and kisses the good-looking babydoll who ain't got much on but a nightgown you can pret-near see through. Man, ain't she the cat's meow, though. She ain't got a *thing* under that nightgown. She don't seem to like that kiss. Good for her! She slaps him acrost the mouth, hard. Now, *he* don't seem to like it. He rubs his hand acrost his jaw and scowls something fierce. And then the caption says he says, 'You'll pay for that, Cynthia.' He grabs her by the shoulders and she ain't got nottin' on them . . ."

One night, the assistant got sick between reels and had to go home. Someone volunteered to take the assistant's place and purposely mixed things up by reporting passionate embraces when the cowboys were chasing Indians, and vice versa. But most people didn't realize what was going on until toward the end, when the pianist played a wedding march while they were burying William S. Hart's bearded and comical old side-kick on Boot Hill.

The Nantucket Quakers would have been shocked speechless by movies. But the Dreamland originally was a Quaker Meeting House, built in 1831 on Main Street. After the Friends all died or disowned each other, the Meeting House became a straw-hat factory and then a skating rink. Next it was moved to Brant Point and became part of the now defunct Nantucket Hotel. And finally it was moved to its present location, where it was a lodge called *Red Men's Hall* before it was made into the movie theater which it is today. The *Red Men* still meet upstairs.

Fortunately for us, Dad was interested in all kinds of photography, and especially in moving pictures. The development of movies had provided a new medium for the study of workers' motions. And just as soon as movie cameras were perfected, Dad had added them to the tools of his trade. He had thousands of feet of film, much of which he had taken himself, showing the best and worst athletes and the best and worst production workers, going through their paces. Dad used to study every detail of their movements so that he could find what he called "the one best way."

So Dad deemed movies to be educational, not because of their plots or the acting but because of such technical details as camera angles and lighting. In all honesty I'll have to admit, though, that Dad often got so engrossed in the plot he forgot all about the photography. And Mother sometimes used to tease him, when the lights came on after a tragic scene and Dad was red-eyed, by asking questions such as:

"Don't you think it would have been better if they had had a backlight shining through her hair hanging over the pillow, when she was dying?"

Sometimes, after my father had taken us to a movie at the Dreamland, we'd walk up Main Street to Congdon's Drug Store for a soda—ice cream and tonic. Then the shortest way home would be along Centre Street, which in the old days was known as Petticoat Row, in honor of the many Quaker women who ran shops there.

At Centre and Quince Streets, there's an old house where Captain George Pollard of the *Essex* lived, back in the 1820's. Everybody on Nantucket knows about Captain Pollard. He's the man who ate his cabin boy, not to mention other assorted members of his crew, both white and colored.

As we'd pass the Pollard house, Dad invariably would recall the *Essex* and speculate in some detail as to which of us would make the most tender dinner, if we were all marooned in an open boat. We'd say, and without any fear of successful contradiction, since Dad weighed some two hundred and fifty pounds, that there was no doubt, at any rate, about who would constitute the *biggest* dinner. But Dad usually chose to ignore remarks about his weight.

"I believe," he would finally conclude, "that if I were starving in a whaleboat the one I'd pick for my first meal would be . . . you-u-u-u-u!"

Then he'd grab one of us, and pick us up, and make believe he was going to sink his teeth into our neck.

It's still dark and scary on the streets of Nantucket at night. Not so dark as it used to be, when the thrifty Quakers exported almost every drop of whale oil, rather than light their own streets. But still dark enough so that Dad's clicking teeth used to make my skin crawl. Mother would scold him for upsetting us—but just the same we liked to steer him past the Pollard house, so that he'd go into his act.

Captain Pollard's ship, the 240-ton *Essex*, was sailing near the Equator in the Pacific at eight o'clock on the morning of November 20, 1820, when the cry of "Thar she blows" went up simultaneously from her three look-outs.

Captain Pollard, spry as a boy, was up mizzen mast ratlines in a matter of seconds, while all hands hit the deck. Pollard, looking through his glass, located a school of whales far off to leeward, and shouted down orders to the helmsman. First Mate Owen Chase prepared to lower three boats. A tense air of excitement gripped the little ship, because a captured whale meant money in everybody's pocket. The crew knew what it was supposed to do, and did it swiftly and well.

As the *Essex* changed course and bore down, the lookouts continued to sing out. "Thar she blows. She blows, blows, blows." Captain Pollard descended to his quarterdeck, and quietly gave the commands.

The *Essex* was hove to about a half mile from the whales.

"Boats," ordered Pollard.

The three whale boats were lowered quickly from their davits. Each was twenty-seven feet long and six feet wide, and manned by five oarsmen and an officer who was the boat steerer.

As customary, only three men—the cooper, the cook, and the cabin boy—were left to sail the *Essex*.

The three open boats shoved off from the mother ship. The water was calm, and the oars left a herringbone wake. Like three centipedes walking on top of the water, the craft closed on their giant prey. The officers at the tillers whispered the rhythm for the oarsmen with the refrain, "A dead whale or a stove boat."

Ordinarily, the bow oar was pulled by a harpooner, who had the status of petty officer aboard ship. The harpooner, invariably a powerful man, would heave his weapon into the whale, and then change places with the boat-steering officer. The harpoon wasn't designed to kill the whale, but only to "hook" it. If everything went right, the monster was killed about an hour after it was "hooked," when it was exhausted from towing the whaleboat around the ocean and from gyrations to rid itself of the painful barb. Once the whale was exhausted, the boat was rowed up along side the monster and the officer in the bow went "after its life" with a lance aimed at the lungs.

Mate Chase, who was as husky as any harpooner, preferred to do his own harpooning as well as lancing. Consequently, when his boat came within striking distance of
the school, he changed places with the man at the bow
oar. Silently—because a sound now could cause the whole
school to dive and disappear—Chase picked up a heavy,
sharp harpoon, connected to the boat with a coiled line
a half-mile long. The first mate fit his thigh into a specially
built clumsy-cleat brace in the bow, and tensed himself
for the important effort.

At this point the thing which always made the biggest
impression on green hands is the fact that, as my brothers
and sisters and I had noticed about the stranded blackfish,
a whale *breathes.* His inhalings and exhalings sound like
those of a giant man. To hear breathing in the middle of
the ocean, where other life exists soundlessly by means
of pumping gills, apparently is an experience that few
men forget. Perhaps, for a moment, Chase and his men
felt a kinship for the huge beast they were about to attack.

The oarsmen, with their backs to the whale, weren't
allowed to look around because there was always a chance
that a view of the whale at close quarters might cause
them to become panicky. Chase motioned with his left
hand that he wanted the boat rowed forward a few feet.
The man at the tiller, also using a hand signal, passed
along the command. The boat edged forward without a
sound.

Some people seem to be under the impression that a
harpooner hurled his weapon javelin-fashion, a hundred
feet or so, in a dramatic arc. Actually, the harpoon was
much too heavy for any such toss. The harpooner used

both hands when he "hove" his weapon, and never tried to throw it more than ten or fifteen feet. In other words, the boat had to come within an oar's length of the whale. At such close quarters, the harpoon seldom missed its mark. The big question, though, was whether the harpoon would hit head-on and whether it would stick.

With a tremendous grunt, Chase hurled the weapon. It sank deep into the back of the female spermaceti, and the big beast leaped instinctively, gulped air, and dived. In the split second that Chase got a look at her tail as she submerged, he made a mental note that she'd be worth four thousand dollars if she was worth a cent.

The rope attached to the harpoon came to life as it snaked out of its coil amidships. The line went from the coil, carefully arranged in a bailing bucket, to a logger-head or post on the gunwale astern. It made one loop around the loggerhead and then came forward through the middle of the boat to a groove in the bow. If a man didn't manage to stay clear of the line, he could lose an arm or a leg.

The men shipped their oars. As the loggerhead began to smoke from the friction of the rope, the man at the tiller sloshed a bucket of water over it. Already, the boat was beginning to move fast enough to kick up a white wake. The oarsmen, dripping sweat and filling their lungs with welcome air, sat back for a moment as they prepared to enjoy the most exciting part of the kill—the Nantucket sleighride, a dashing, spray-eating spin across the ocean at speeds reaching twenty-five miles an hour; speeds faster than any person in the world, except a whaling man, had ever traveled on water.

The men in Chase's boat didn't get to enjoy their sleigh-ride.

The line suddenly slacked off. For a moment or two, it seemed as if the harpoon must have pulled free. But then there was a bump and a terrifying lurch, as the whale surfaced under the boat and, with a flip of its tail, punched a hole in the side. Then the animal sounded.

Chase took one look at the damage. In a split-second decision, he seized a hatchet which was kept in the bow for just such an emergency, and cut the line.

Miraculously, no one was hurt. Some of the men stuffed their jackets into the hole. Chase took over the tiller again, and gave orders to row back to the *Essex*.

When they were safely aboard the vessel once more, the mate supervised the repair of the whaleboat, and watched through his telescope the activity of the captain's and the second mate's boats. The captain's boat finally harpooned a whale. The school had moved somewhat to westward and leeward, and Chase half-sailed half-drifted the *Essex* in that direction.

Suddenly a huge sperm bull, much bigger than the female which had smashed their whaleboat, surfaced off the bow of the *Essex*, blew twice, and lazily sank again. A few seconds later, the whale came up again about a ship's length off. The bull studied the *Essex* through eyes not much bigger than a man's, and for some unexplained reason exploded into a foaming, frenzied rage. Slapping the water with a ponderous tail, the enraged beast headed for the ship.

Never before in the whole history of whaling had a whale *deliberately* charged a ship, although ships had bumped into whales accidentally and of course whales had attacked the tiny, open whaleboats.

In amazement that amounted to disbelief, Mate Chase roared orders to the helmsman.

The whole horror story of what followed was subsequently recorded by the survivors down to the last detail. Chase himself wrote the most thorough and dramatic account, and got to press with it first. His version was published in 1821, a month or two after he got back to Nantucket. Unlike many authors, Chase admitted frankly that he wrote his booklet for money. In the preface, he pointed out that he had lost most of his belongings at sea. Then he added that he had composed the booklet "in the hope of obtaining something of remuneration by giving a short history of my sufferings to the world."

Chase wrote that his orders to the helmsman came too late. The ship changed course as the man at the wheel veered off. But the huge bull changed course with the ship, and homed in like the radar-controlled torpedoes of today.

There was a splintering crash as the beast rammed his jaws into the *Essex*, near the forechains. The ship brought up violently as if she had hit a rock.

"We realized at once the dreadful accident which had befallen us," Chase wrote in the stilted language of the day. "After recovering in a measure from the consternation that had seized us, I concluded that the whale had stove a hole in the ship."

The First Mate set the men to work on the pumps, and ordered a signal hoisted on the foremast to recall the whaleboats of the Captain and the Second Mate.

Meanwhile, Chase kept an anxious eye out for the rogue whale. And after a few minutes the whale emerged a hundred yards to leeward, shaking his head as if he were stunned. Then, apparently regaining control of his faculties and seeing the *Essex* again, the whale started "smiting his jaws together in rage and fury," Chase recorded.

Chase had to race forward to see how the pumps were doing. Then the hairs on his neck stood on end as he heard the helmsman shriek:

"Here he is. He's making for us again."

Chase came aft, and while he and his men gaped in terror, the rogue struck under the cathead and completely stove in the bow.

"He passed under the ship again, went off leeward, and we never saw him again," wrote the First Mate.

What was to follow was even more terrifying. But as many readers already will have perceived, the fate of the *Essex* parallels closely the last heroic chapter of *Moby Dick*. Indeed, the attack on a whaleship by a rogue whale is the basic plot of *Moby Dick*, which was written thirty years later. A copy of Chase's booklet, with Melville's penciled notes on the margin, is a collector's item today. Had it not been for what happened to the *Essex*, Melville probably would have rejected as implausible the thought that his great white whale, Moby Dick, could sink the *Pequod*. Whales had been known to swim along with ships and scratch their backs by brushing almost affectionately across the ships' bottoms—as a dog will do to the underside of a chair. But prior to the *Essex* episode, a sailor would have guffawed at the thought of a whale deliberately sinking a ship.

The *Essex* filled with water in a matter of minutes. Just before she shivered and toppled over on her beam ends, Chase managed to launch the spare whaleboat, while his men grabbed the two compasses from the binnacle and two quadrants from the table in the officers' mess.

The *Essex* was on her side, with Chase and the men sitting in the whaleboat, when Captain Pollard and Second Mate Matthew P. Joy steered their boats up to the wreck. Chase wrote that the Captain remarked:

"My God, Mr. Chase, what has happened."

"We have been stove by a whale," replied Chase.

Reassuming command, Pollard ordered the ship's three masts chopped away, so that she could right herself. When she finally did so, with her decks awash, the crew hacked through the planking and salvaged Pollard's and Chase's sea chests, six hundred pounds of bread, tinter boxes, some fresh water, and a couple of live turtles from the Galápagos Islands. Among the contents of Chase's chest were paper and pencils, on which for a time he made notes for his subsequent booklet. There were three pistols in the Captain's chest, as well as a number of other useful articles.

After the crew had salvaged what it could, Pollard, Chase, and Joy held a whispered conference in the Captain's boat about what course they should sail to try to make land. There were no accurate charts of the area, and Pollard decided that the safest procedure would be to head for South America, some 2,500 miles away! It was agreed that the three boats would remain together, if possible.

And so the three officers and seventeen men, with tiny

sails pulling their open boats, set out on a voyage which for endurance and seamanship made maritime history.

After about two weeks at sea, the boats were so battered that all three were leaking, and the men were so weak from short rations that they could scarcely bail. One of the turtles was killed then, pried loose from its shell, and cooked over a fire built within the shell. The men ate every scrap of it, and then eagerly drank the blood.

This gave them renewed strength for a few days—and they needed it, because a fierce storm struck and every man had to bail for his life, while being tossed around on the bottoms as the boats jolted from wave to wave. They were wet all the time, either from spray or from water in the bottoms of the boats or from both. The salt rotted off their clothes, and the men blistered in the sun. Festering boils formed where the salt rubbed into the blisters. But the men managed to stay alive and to keep the three boats together.

When the winds died down to a flat calm, some of the men sought to ease the pain of the blisters and boils by sliding over the side and soaking themselves in the sea, while hanging onto the gunwales. They discovered that the bottoms of the boats were covered with little clam-like barnacles. Within a matter of minutes, every shellfish was clawed loose and devoured.

A few flying fish hit the sails and dropped into the boats. They were gobbled down—bones, scales, and all—by whoever was lucky enough to grab them. The food from the *Essex* now had dwindled to the point where it could be locked in the sea chests. At night, the officers slept lying over the chests, with pistols in their hands.

On December 16, twenty-six days after the *Essex* was sunk, the officers cut all rations in half. Since there hadn't been a breath of wind for three days, the men tried to row. But they were too weak to make much headway.

The following day, however, a good wind sprang up, and on December 20, a small island was sighted. Babbling hysterically, the men rowed to it.

The island turned out to be small and practically barren. There were a few birds' eggs, a few young birds and some shellfish, which they ate eagerly. They even managed to catch a few fish. After two days of exploration, they found a small spring of fresh water, which became exposed only at low tide.

But within three days, everything edible had been consumed. And the spring was yielding barely enough water to keep them alive. So the boats were hauled up on the shore and repaired, and fourteen men and the officers set sail again December 27. Three men elected to remain on Ducie's Island, as the barren spot is now known. Captain Pollard agreed that there probably was enough food and water on the island to sustain three people.

Because storms had driven the boats southward instead of to the southeast, Captain Pollard estimated that they still had 2,500 miles to go, to reach South America. They had four casks of water, painstakingly filled on the island, and a small amount of bread husbanded from the *Essex*.

Now the nightmarish horrors came in quick succession. Lips parched by the tropic sun swelled frightfully, cracked open, and became infected. At night, the bearded skeletons huddled together wet and miserable on the bottoms of the boats, trying to draw animal warmth from each other.

On January 10, Second Mate Joy died from a combination of exposure and starvation. They sewed his body in what was left of his clothes and pushed him over the side. Chase wrote that the burial was conducted in a "solemn manner."

Two days later, Chase himself had grown so weak and forgetful that he neglected to lock his sea chest. One of the seamen stole a piece of bread from the chest, but before the man could stuff it in his mouth Chase pulled himself together enough to force the man to return it—at pistol point.

That same night, a sudden tropical squall swept down on the boats, and it was every man for himself to keep the little shells afloat. At dawn the next day, Chase and his crew could find no sign of the other two boats. Since misery loves company, Chase and his four men broke into bitter tears.

January 20, a Negro crewman named Richard Peterson died in Chase's boat, and was pushed over the side in a "solemn manner." Then on February 8, when the men were literally starving, Isaac Cole, another seaman, went raving, gibbering mad. Cole sat up in the bottom of the boat and demanded not only food and water, but a napkin. They tried to quiet him, but his demands became more shrill and insistent. It was, Chase wrote, "a most miserable spectacle of madness." The First Mate added:

"We covered him with some old clothes and left him to his fate. He lay in the greatest pain and apparent misery, groaning piteously until 4 o'clock, when he died in the most horrid and frightful convulsions I ever witnessed."

That left Chase and two men. And now there was only enough bread for three days. Probably the thought went through everyone's mind at the same time. If Cole could be considered as provisions, they could stay alive for another couple of weeks.

While his two men were preparing Cole for burial, Chase put the suggestion into words. He didn't have to twist the arm of either of his live crewmen. He wrote that the three of them fell to "as fast was we were able," and feasted.

Readers with queasy stomachs may want to skip the next two paragraphs. Chase recorded that:

"We separated his limbs from his body, cut off all the flesh, took out the heart, sewed up the remains in canvas, and committed it to the deep. Making a fire, we partook of Isaac and preserved his remainder for future use . . . The next morning, we found the flesh spoiling and made a fire and cooked it. For five or six days we lived on it, not using our remnant of bread."

The First Mate added piously in his booklet that, "Humanity shudders at the recital," and that the very thought of eating Isaac "brings to my mind some of the most revolting ideas that it is capable of conceiving."

After Isaac was gone but not forgotten, Chase and the two men ate what was left of the bread. Finally there was nothing at all to eat in the boat except the three living human beings.

"We did not know to whose lot it would fall next either to die or be shot," Chase wrote.

The three must have sat eying each other hungrily, although Chase didn't say so. He implied, in fact, rather the opposite. He said that on February 17, when seventeen-year-old Thomas Nicholson announced that he was going to die, Chase himself tried to encourage him to keep living.

"I endeavored to convince him that it was wicked to abandon reliance on Providence while the last hope remained," wrote the Mate. "But he felt unwilling to listen to my consolatory suggestions."

Nicholson lay down in the boat, pulled a piece of canvas over him, said he didn't care who ate him, and prepared to meet his Maker.

And then in a climax almost too good to be true, the other crewman, Benjamin Lawrence, stood up in the boat, waved a skeleton's arm, and croaked, "Sail ho."

"Where away," Chase responded calmly and automatically, a sailor to the end. With a double-take, he too climbed unsteadily to his feet and shrieked, "Where? Where? Where?"

Even Nicholson, giving up the idea of dying and thrusting aside the canvas, managed to pull himself up to the gunwale.

The ship, the brig *Indian* out of London, was about seven miles away, and she quickly changed course. An hour later, when she maneuvered alongside the whaleboat, the survivors had collapsed on the bottom—three hairy, almost-naked bags of bones, covered with boils and sores, their glazed, staring eyes sunk back into their skulls.

They cooed and gurgled baby-like while they were lifted aboard and put to bed. For three days, they couldn't keep down anything but tapioca soup.

They had sailed a total of 3,700 miles, on two legs of a

journey which had brought them to within less than three
hundred miles of the South American coast. On Febuary
25, the *Indian* landed them at Valparaiso, Chile, and they
were soon ready to go to sea again.

Nothing was ever heard of Second Mate Joy's whaleboat. But Captain Pollard made it back all right, with one
crewman. Neither Pollard nor the crewman, Charles Ramsdell, liked to talk about their experiences. But the story
finally leaked out in some of its grisly detail.

Pollard and his five crewmen ate all their supplies before the first man died. He was a Negro, and they ate
him. Then a second Negro died, and they ate him, too.

Pollard and the three men waited patiently until February 1 for someone else to die. When nobody obliged, they
drew lots to see who would be killed.

The young cabin boy, Owen Coffin, drew the short lot.
Owen was a nephew of Captain Pollard, and Pollard of-
fered to take the boy's place as the human sacrifice. But
Owen bravely insisted on paying his own gambling debts.

While Owen said his prayers, the other three—Pollard,
Charles Ramsdell and Barzillai Ray—drew lots again to
see who would execute him. Ramsdell, a boy in his teens
and a close friend of Owen's, drew the short lot. Ramsdell
then begged Owen to trade places with him, thrusting a
pistol into Owen's hands and urging Owen to shoot him.
But Owen still insisted on his "right" to die.

The cabin boy leaned his head over the gunwale, so
that the spent bullet wouldn't pierce the boat. Ramsdell
put the pistol to Owen's head, closed his eyes, and fired.

They ate Owen for ten days, and then Barzillai Ray

died—while there was still some of Owen left. Pollard and Ramsdell were gnawing on the bones when they were picked up February 23 off St. Mary's Island, Chile, by the Nantucket whaling ship *Dauphin.*

A member of the *Dauphin* crew, Charles Murphey of Nantucket, wrote a long "epic poem" about the rescue, in a journal which he kept of his voyage. After telling how Pollard and Ramsdell were carried aboard the *Dauphin,* Murphey penned dolorously:

> The rest belonging to the boat
> Ah! Shocking tale to relate,
> For want of food and nourishment
> Met an unhappy fate.

The *Dauphin* arrived in Valparaiso March 17, 1821—three weeks after Chase, Nicholson and Lawrence had been put ashore there. All five of the survivors were Nantucketers, and they had "as joyful a reunion as could be expected under the unusual circumstances."

Pollard arranged for the English ship *Surrey,* which was leaving Valparaiso for Australia, to stop off at Dulcie's Island and pick up the other three men. They were rescued April 8, and one of them wrote an account of his experiences. However, since none of the three was a Nantucketer, the account isn't particularly pertinent to this story.

The five Nantucketers returned home from Valparaiso aboard the whaleship *Hero,* which flew the black flag of disaster—a signal of death—from her masthead as she entered Nantucket harbor. Almost everyone on the island crowded down to the wharfs to hear the news. Word of what had happened in the *Essex* whaleboats was quickly whispered from group to group. Women burst into tears. As the survivors stepped ashore, the crowd pushed back and opened aisles through its midst, allowing the five cannibals to file silently to their homes. Pollard and his men kept their heads high, and looked straight ahead.

It shouldn't be deduced, though, that the *Essex* survivors were placed in Coventry or that they even lost any standing in the community. Being a seafaring town, Nantucket understood the rigid hardships which the sea sometimes imposes. And in fact Pollard and Chase both gained prestige because of their remarkable jobs of navigation and of keeping their whaleboats afloat.

All five of the survivors soon went to sea again, and all eventually became captains—except of course, Pollard, who already was one.

Although Chase himself wrote of his experiences, most other Nantucketers were reluctant to discuss the *Essex* episode—particularly to discuss it with off-islanders. The cannibalism apparently was regarded as a sort of family tragedy that one did not care to mention.

For instance, Obed Macy's history written fourteen years after the return of the survivors stressed the "astonishment" that a whale attacked the *Essex* and marveled at the endurance and seamanship of the survivors, all of whom Macy knew personally.

But when it came to their cannibalism, he was tactfully oblique. He pointed out merely that after their bread was all but gone and one of their number died of starvation, they "determined to extend their indulgence and take the consequences, whether to live or die."

There are a number of sequels to the story of the *Essex*. Captain Pollard went to sea again in November of that same year, as master of the whaleship *Two Brothers*. Five months later, through no fault of his own, he wrecked her on an uncharted reef—which now bears his name— west of the Sandwich Islands. Again he and his crew had to take to the ocean in whaleboats. But if the more corpulent members of his new crew dreaded to make such a voyage with a captain who had eaten his cabin boy and three other "hands" the dread was short-lived. For within three days, they were rescued by the Nantucket whaler *Martha*.

After having lost two ships through bad luck, Pollard figured he was a jinx, and so did the ship-owners. So he "swallowed the anchor," as the expression went, and never set sail again. He remained a respectable citizen of Nantucket, though, and served for years as a member of the town's watch in a capacity akin to that of policeman. He died at the age of eighty-one, and got a nice writeup in *The Nantucket Inquirer and Mirror*, which didn't mention cannibalism.

Chase became one of Nantucket's best-known whaling captains. After he retired, he lived in a snug, gray house which still stands at York and Orange Streets. They say on Nantucket that Chase never let a single crumb be wasted either at his home or aboard his ships. As a bent old man, a terror of starvation came back to him and he'd secretly smuggle home extra food from the market, in his greatcoat pockets. When no one around the house was looking, he'd tiptoe to the attic and hide the food under the eaves.

A favorite story which is contained in almost every

book on Nantucket involves the time that a young reporter from a New Bedford or Boston paper came to the island to interview old whaling captains. The reporter happened to be a descendant of one of the Nantucket families, and among those he interviewed was old Captain Owen Chase.

At the conclusion of the interview, which had touched only on general matters, the reporter said:

"By the way, sir, perhaps you knew one of my great uncles. His name was Isaac Cole, and I understand he died in a whaleboat in the Pacific."

"Know him?" cackled Chase. "Know him? Why, son, I *et* him."

It is more than a coincidence that when I checked on the *Hero*, in connection with the *Essex* story, I discovered that she also had just figured in quite an adventure. The point is that the early whaling ships almost *always* had adventures.

When Chase, Pollard and the other three survivors boarded the *Hero* at Valparaiso, they found that a sixteen-year-old Nantucket boy, Obed Starbuck, was her acting captain.

Obed was thirteen when he first went to sea, and his cruise with the *Hero* was his second voyage. The *Hero* had left Nantucket at about the same time as the *Essex*. She was commanded by Captain James Russell, and she had had a successful voyage until she started to head back home from the Pacific.

Like most whaleships, she planned to put in at Valparaiso for provisions and repairs, before the dangerous

homeward trip around Cape Horn. But she was boarded
and captured near St. Mary's Island, off the Chile coast,
by a band of cutthroats led by the notorious pirate Captain Benevedes.

The pirate took the ship to nearby Arauco, Chile, where
he ordered the crew ashore. Then he shot and killed Captain Russell and the cabin boy. That night, Obed escaped
from his guards, rallied some members of the crew, recaptured the *Hero,* and sailed her to Valparaiso, three
hundred miles to the north.

When the sixteen-year-old boy subsequently brought
the *Hero* back home to Nantucket with the *Essex* survivors, the owners came aboard, shook hands with him,
and called him "Captain" Starbuck. That was their way
of informing him that he'd be in command of the *Hero,*
when she next went to sea.

Their confidence in him was well justified, because Obed
Starbuck became one of the most successful whaling captains of his generation. Starbuck was the master of the
Loper which, as mentioned before, set a record in 1829
by returning to Nantucket from the Pacific with a full
cargo of oil worth $50,000, after a voyage of only fourteen
months. He discovered fifteen or twenty important Pacific
islands, among them Starbuck Island and New Nantucket
(now Baker) Island. The plain but handsome house he
built in 1831, near the corner of Fair and School Streets,
is now known as the *Ship's Inn.*

8. DUSKY DEBUTANTES

Our mailman at Nantucket was an ordinarily cheerful man named John Conway. He liked children and, although he couldn't tell us apart, it had intrigued him to learn all of our names.

He made his rounds on foot twice a day, and as he approached our house he'd sing out, "Annie and Ernie and Martie and Frankie. Martie and Frankie and Billie and Lillie. Billie and Lillie and Freddie and Dannie." When subsequent children arrived and Mr. Conway got older, he chose, for some reason, to ignore the new names and to substitute in their stead some names that he pulled out of thin air. His chanted song remained accurate as to the first eight of us, but then he'd launch into fiction with "Ichabod and Mertie and Whozie and Cornelius. Whozie and Cornelius and Claudie and Maudie. Claudie and

Maudie and Whatzie and Sammie." And so forth, at such length that anyone would have thought we were four dozen children, instead of a single dozen.

When we tried to correct him as to the names of the new arrivals, he'd ignore us, and sing all the louder.

Since our cottage and lighthouses were a block closer to the beach than any other house in the vicinity, Mr. Conway's route was lengthened somewhat by our arrival. Also, to get to our house, he had to walk along a sandy road where the going always was pretty rough. And, finally, there was the matter of the bulk of our mail. Mr. Conway used to say that we got almost as much mail as the combined total of everyone else on the route.

Mr. Conway never complained about any of this. I'm sure he figured that it was all a part of his job—and let it go at that. But it may have explained why—in mild and subconscious rebellion against being our drayhorse—he chose eventually to substitute a long string of fictitious names for the actual names of our latest arrivals.

Dad's magazines comprised a large portion of our daily mail. He liked to keep up with everything written about Motion Study and Management, both in this country and abroad. As a result, he subscribed to thirty or forty bulky and technical publications ranging from *Iron Age* to *Factory*—actually not much of a range, when you come right down to it.

Also, as a part of his program to supplement our education in public schools, he subscribed to quite a few magazines such as *Esperanto, The Literary Digest,* and *The National Geographic Magazine.* Of all of these, I found the *Geographic* to be by far the most enlightening.

Although I have made no survey comparable to Dr. Kinsey's, I am ready to report just the same that the pristine *Geographic*, with its yellow-bordered cover as chaste as any daffodil, contributed vastly to the sex education of many boys born during the early half of this century. I have recently interviewed a number of my contemporaries on this subject, and in almost every case their eyes have lit up and they have reached across the desk to nudge me.

"Those South Sea Island girls dressed only in a G-string," they whisper happily out of the sides of their mouths, becoming for an instant enthusiastic but somewhat shamefaced boys again. "Wow."

In those days, pictures of thin-clad, semi-clad, and unclad females did not adorn the pages of general magazines. And even at the bathing beaches, where black stockings and tent-like swimming suits were *de rigueur*, it was not possible for a young boy to observe with any degree of certainty wherein the female form differed from that of his own.

But in the *Geographic*, some of the basic differences protruded in bold, if dusky, relief.

Sometimes after supper at Nantucket, while Mother put the babies to bed, we'd sit around the dining room table and Dad would go through his magazines and read us excerpts from various pieces he considered to be "educational."

But when it came to the *Geographic*, Dad was inclined to give extremely short shrift to the interestingly illustrated articles about natives of Africa and the South Seas; and to give hours and hours of shrift to articles on such safe subjects as expeditions to Tibet, hunting rams with a camera in the Canadian Rockies, and fishing for cod off the coast of Nova Scotia.

In fact, Dad was as prim and reluctant as any Quaker about discussing with his children either the human form or sex—and didn't want any part of any such discussion. My older sisters, realizing this, never commented on the way he ignored the articles on the natives. But one of my younger brothers was less inhibited.

"How come," he asked Dad one night, "you always skip all those good pictures of the funny colored people in their birthday suits with the white paint on and with the ears that hang down past their shoulders?"

Dad cleared his throat loudly, and made believe he didn't hear. "Now this," he said, "is an *extremely* interesting new map of Chile. Someone help me unfold it. That's it. Now, you see, when the Nantucket whaling ships started to come back home, they'd land right here at Valparaiso. I'll bet a nickel none of you can tell me what Chile's second largest city is?"

"I'll bet a nickel, Daddy," said the persistent young brother, "that you'd sure look funny if you were in your birthday suit and all painted up like those colored people, eh Daddy?"

Somebody tittered, and Dad blushed.

"I guess I would," Dad was honest enough to admit. "But getting back to Chile . . ."

Someone tittered again.

"All right," Dad said glumly, "I'll go ahead and make the obvious joke before somebody else does. If I were in my birthday suit like those colored people, I'd be *chilly*, too.

Now let's get back to the *country* of Chile and see if we can't learn something. Who knows what the second largest city . . ."

"Why do some of those colored people have ears that hang down past their shoulders?" my brother interrupted.

I suppose Dad realized that there wasn't any use going on with Chile until he had cleared up some of the questions about the savages. He sighed and gave his undivided attention to the brother.

"What do you mean?" asked Dad.

"Like in this picture here," said my brother, taking the magazine and turning to the article in question. The illustration showed two male savages with stretched ears and two extremely buxom females who had nothing on above the waist. Even though the ears were gigantic, I found it difficult to concentrate entirely on them.

"Man, look at those great big ears, eh Daddy?" said my brother.

"Yes, *sir*," Dad acknowledged, blushing again. "Those are some of the biggest ears I ever saw."

He was about to turn the page, but my brother was a stubborn youngster.

"Does it say how their ears got so big, Daddy?"

"Oh, they used to stretch their ears," said Dad. "The men thought that having stretched ears made them very handsome. Now let's see, getting back to Chile . . ."

"That's why the men stretched their chests, too, like these two fellows over here, eh Daddy?" said my brother, pointing to the two women. "I'll bet they thought that a stretched chest made them handsome, too."

Nobody giggled this time, and Dad now turned crimson.

"Maybe so," he agreed tentatively.

"Those things would be pretty handy for baseball, eh Daddy? If you were catching behind the plate, you wouldn't have to wear a chest protector or anything except a mask."

"Like fun you wouldn't," one of my young sisters put in.

Dad banged the table with the magazine. "No more interruptions," he ordered. "Where's the map of Chile. Where was I? Oh, yes, what's the second largest . . ."

Suddenly, he stopped, gurgled, dropped the magazine, yanked off his *pince nez*, and exploded through his nose in an uncontrollable bellow of laughter. Apparently deciding there wasn't any use to try to hold it back and that the harm, anyway, had been done, he put his arms on the table and his head on his arms and roared so that he shook the whole table. Some of the younger ones didn't know what the joke was, but everybody joined in.

"Lord, boy," Dad wheezed, finally coming up for air and wiping his eyes with the back of his hand, "you're going to be the death of me yet." He reached over and rumpled my young brother's hair. "I ache all over. Phew. Where's that map of Chile, now, and no more nonsense."

Dad may have been embarrassed to discuss with us the physical attributes of the *Geographic*'s natives, but at least he didn't object to our studying the pictures by ourselves —just as long as he wasn't around.

He and Mother were considerably more broadminded in that attitude than the parents of a friend of mine who lived up on The Cliff at Nantucket. My friend's parents subscribed to the *Geographic,* too. But they cut out and destroyed certain illustrations, before they left the magazine where he could see it. Naturally, when he came to our house, he could hardly wait to check through our copy, to get filled in on what his parents had censored.

"They must think I'm a *child,*" he'd tell me, while turning with lip-licking eagerness from one uncensored page to the next. "A child! Gracious Gawd, Frank, look at *her!*"

If mere pictures of South Sea Island debutantes disturbed boys in the Twentieth Century, it's not difficult to imagine that the debutantes themselves, in the flesh, made an impact on Nantucket boys—and men too—a hundred and fifty years ago.

Nantucket whalemen became the foremost authorities on the Pacific aborigines. But you can be sure that the stories the whalemen brought home were carefully censored. A Quaker man, married to a woman so prim that she even wore a bonnet to bed, couldn't allow himself to describe in much detail the sinuous, satin-skinned native girls who sometimes greeted him quite literally with open arms. And he figured that the less said at home the better, about the shocking purpose for which some pleasure-loving chiefs kept, in addition to their wives, groups of growing boys.

A good many people today have an entirely inaccurate conception of life on the Pacific Islands before the white men came. The early missionaries, who were concerned principally with putting clothes on the savages and stopping them from committing adultery, are partly responsible for this misconception. The missionaries had the problem of raising money at home for their uplifting work, and I guess they didn't want to picture the savages as too hopelessly immoral to be uplifted. Also, like the Nantucket whalemen, the missionaries found that there were certain customs on the islands which couldn't very well be described to the Ladies Bible Class back home.

So the missionaries created the impression that, aside from going naked, there was very little vice among the simple savages. The missionaries conceded that of course there was some cannibalism, but they added the cannibalism wasn't particularly widespread, and that where it *did* occur, it was mostly a religious rite.

The missionaries probably believed sincerely themselves that if they could put pants on the men and skirts on the women, all the adultery would stop; and that, if they could abolish all the old religious rites and make Christians out of the savages, there would be no more cannibalism.

But the facts are that whether or not they were made to wear clothes, the natives didn't understand what adultery was. And while cannibalism was tied in with certain religious rites, it existed principally for this basic reason that had nothing to do with religion: Many of the natives thought that of all meats, human flesh—long pig—was the most delicious.

Some of the more moral of the Nantucket whaling captains occasionally tried themselves to do missionary work among the natives, and even attempted to translate the Ten Commandments into various native tongues. But they ran into an impasse when it came to translating the commandment about adultery, because there wasn't any such

native word. On the Sandwich Islands, the best that anyone could come up with was, "Thou shalt not engage in
mischievous sleeping." And that translation left the natives completely mystified.

Americans stationed on Pacific islands during World
War II may also have contributed unknowingly to mis-
conceptions about the natives. Our men found the natives
on some of the islands to be scaly, diseased, filthy creatures, devoid of courage and self-respect.

But that's not the way the natives were when the first
Nantucketers came. Back in those days, the savages were
strong, healthy, handsome, and brave. It was only after
being subjected to the civilization of the whites that the
savages became diseased. There is an all-too-obvious paral-
lel here with the fate of the American Indians.

For instance, on the Marquesan Islands south of Hawaii,
the death rate over the last hundred years has been ap-
palling. But when the first Nantucketers arrived there, disease was practically unknown. The men were six feet tall
and more, muscular, fearless, cruel to their victims, and
yet basically easy going and good natured. They had perfect teeth, fine features, and clear skin. The women were
lovely—proud, slender, and graceful, with luxuriant,
slightly waved black hair that hung to their waists.

The Marquesan men were cannibals and inveterate
gamblers, and their favorite recreations were committing
adultery, drinking home brew, and torturing prisoners.
They'd bet anything from a canoe to a wife on who could
win a footrace or catch the most fish. Some of their erotic
orgies, in the form of dances not unlike the hula, continued for three days and nights, with the exhausted

participants occasionally dropping out to rest and then gamely rejoining the festivities.

When the Marquesan men ate long pig, they offered the eyes and some other tidbits to their god, Tiki. But otherwise there was no religious connection. Before engaging in battle, they screwed up their courage and whetted their appetite by singing a song to the effect that, "This is a time when men are fat."

Most of the persons eaten were members of rival tribes, killed or captured in battle. And when there was a big slaughter, the victorious tribe proudly presented some of the cadavers to friendly neighbors, much as an American today would share a big catch of fish.

When there weren't any wars and they ran out of captives, fellow tribesmen would eat each other. Usually a chief designated which of his followers were to be killed, and of course he picked the men he liked the least. It paid to stand in well with your group leader. Women never were allowed to practice cannibalism, and most tribes wouldn't eat their own women. But women of other tribes were eaten with relish.

As for marital habits, a Marquesan boy and girl lived together for two weeks on a honeymoon, and then an older man moved in and shared the wife. The savages didn't understand what was meant by spiritual love for a woman or desire to become her exclusive possessor. No child ever knew who his father was, so the children were cared for by the entire community. A child might sleep for a couple of days in one hut, and then move on to another for a few days. The children were so well loved that they became pretty badly spoiled.

But the Marquesans were wicked to prisoners, including children. Captured children might be dangled feet first from the mast of a returning canoe and allowed to swing, like the clappers of a bell-buoy, until their brains were mashed. Some natives were extraordinarily fond of brains, and would scoop them out coconut-fashion from the top of a crushed skull. Adult captives often were tortured horribly before they were eaten. There was one old chief who used to enjoy cutting off a captive's arm, munching on it raw, and then slapping the captive with the severed arm and telling him that his meat was not only tough but had a revolting flavor.

At first the Nantucket whaling men sometimes were greeted as gods by the savages. Naturally, the white men enjoyed playing that role, and they usually abused it. They'd start out by letting the natives hear their watches tick and by urging them to look at themselves in little hand mirrors. Then perhaps one of the "gods" would shoot off a musket with a deafening roar at a bird standing on the beach. When the bird dropped dead, the natives would fall flat on the ground and roll their eyes in wonder.

But the original awe in which white men were held changed very soon to a contempt bred of familiarity. This was especially true in those instances when the sailors would get full of native booze, push around the warriors, go blundering into the chiefs' huts, commit nuisances on sacred and tabooed ground, and chase down every naked girl in sight.

The shrewd captains, meanwhile, would be stocking their ships with water, bananas, coconuts, and other provisions, for which they promised to pay the chiefs. But sometimes the captains "paid with the fore-topsail"—an all too common practice of promising everything, and then sailing away in the middle of the night without paying anything.

The broken promises and wild debauches were far less common among the Quaker-bred Nantucket whalemen than among the crews from other ports. But to the natives, who didn't know Nantucket from London or Lisbon, a white man was a white man.

The whalemen, too, sometimes made the mistake of thinking there were no differences among the various native tribes. Actually, no two tribes were alike.

At one island, the native girls might make it immediately plain that they thought all white men were wonderful. By uninhibited gestures which must have made a Quaker's eyes pop, the girls would surmount the language barrier almost immediately. To repulse the girls, who placed no more moral significance on love-making than Nantucket girls placed on shaking hands, was to run the risk of offending not only them, but their chief as well.

Yet at an island only a few hundred miles away, the girls might be revolted by the bearded faces and white skins of the visitors. Or the warriors and chief might get fighting mad if a woman was so much as touched under any circumstances.

Having been entertained to the point of erotic exhaustion by the jolly girls at the first island, a whaleman might display impatience and annoyance when the girls at the second island scorned and eluded him. It didn't seem at all logical to him that on one island the girls couldn't get enough affection and that at the next island the girls had screaming hysterics when he chased them into the bushes.

Because of the dangers involved, if not for the moral welfare of their crews, most Nantucket whaling masters would have preferred to steer clear of the islands altogether, if that had been possible. But when fresh water and provisions got low, it was absolutely necessary to stop somewhere.

But where? The Black Islands of Melanesia, where the ferocious warriors chewed betel nut and filed their teeth into points, were to be avoided if at all possible. But sometimes they, too, had to be visited, if water casks were dry.

When a ship dropped anchor in the lagoon of an uncharted island, the first question in everyone's mind was whether the island was inhabited, and the second question was whether the inhabitants liked white meat. The first question was usually answered immediately, because if the natives were there they customarily swarmed around the ship. The second question might not be answered for days, until the terrible moment when the whalemen were seized, stripped, and led to the boiling pots or baking ovens. For the natives were shrewd, and knew it was easy to capture an enemy when he was off guard—after he had been sated with food, drink, and women.

The fact that natives greeted a ship with broad smiles and bunches of bananas was no sign that they weren't planning a big feast of long pig. So it was difficult for a captain to decide, when the natives first started climbing over the sides of his ship, whether he should welcome them or tell his men to repel them with harpoons and blubber knives.

Even when an honest, moral captain steered his ship to

an island where he had previously been treated hospitably, there was no guarantee he would be welcomed a second time. There was always the chance that on his earlier visit his men had spread a disease that broke out after their departure, or that the island had subsequently been visited by a captain who paid with the fore-topsail.

It's a mistake to try to generalize about the Pacific natives, and there were exceptions to every rule which the whalemen tried to apply to them. Some captains were always welcomed like brothers on certain islands, and had native wives to whom they returned every few years. Some tribes, for no apparent reason, would eat all the members of one crew, but a few weeks later show the greatest kindness and consideration to a shipwrecked sailor.

The most dreaded islands of all were the Fijis in Melanesia. And yet a Nantucket boy, William S. Cary, lived there like a king for years. When he came home, he wrote an exciting if stilted narrative of his experiences, and managed to soft-pedal sex to such an extent that the reader is almost—but not quite—led to believe that William was a celibate.

The narrative was lost for a time, but then turned up somehow or other in a fishing shack in 'Sconset, and was published serially in *The Nantucket Journal* about seventy years ago. More about that in the next thrilling chapter.

Perhaps because they were afraid their men wouldn't behave themselves with the native girls, a few Nantucket wives eventually insisted on accompanying their seacaptain husbands into the Pacific. Or perhaps I'm not being fair—the women may have insisted on making the voyages because they loved their husbands so much they couldn't bear to be separated from them.

One of the first Nantucket females to go to sea was a vivacious and headstrong girl named Nancy Wyer Grant. She was only sixteen when she married Captain Charles Grant, and after he returned from a whaling voyage four years later she told him:

"I won't be left alone again, lashed to the kitchen halyards. Next time, I'm going with thee."

Grant thought it was a pretty good idea himself, but the owner of his ship objected strongly. Nevertheless, Nancy had her way, and she was aboard on the captain's next cruise to the Pacific in 1849.

Nancy was a good sport, and only occasionally caused her husband any inconvenience. Of course, Grant *did* have to put into Pitcairn Island, so that a midwife could help Nancy have her first baby. But four months later, Nancy more than made up for that by sighting a whale.

The Grants' first baby, Charles Jr., was delivered by Annie Christian, who said she was a daughter of Fletcher Christian, the Bounty mutineer. The only complaint Nancy made about Pitcairn was a minor one. She had a terrible craving for "good, white bread," and there wasn't any on the island.

Meanwhile, Grant had been looking for whales—and hadn't found a single one. After he stopped at Pitcairn to pick up Nancy and his new son, he offered a twenty-dollar goldpiece to the first person who sighted a whale.

Apparently the lookouts went to sleep at the switch just the same, because Nancy was out on deck one morning, hanging up young Charles' diapers on the ratlines, when she looked out at the horizon and unmistakably saw the "blow" of a whale. She dropped the wash and almost swallowed two clothespins, as she hollered, "Thar she blows." The whale was captured, and Nancy punched a hole in her goldpiece and wore it around her neck for luck.

It's a well-known superstition that women are supposed to bring bad luck to sailing ships. But Mrs. Grant brought her husband nothing but greasy luck, and he became one of the most successful skippers in the whaling business.

On later voyages, Mrs. Grant had a couple of more babies—Eleanor was born on the Bay of Islands, New Zealand, and George at Upolo, Samoa. Then she missed a voyage, but after about a year she got so lonesome for Captain Grant that she left the two older children with her mother and booked passage with young George from Nantucket to Australia.

In Australia, she got word that Grant was in New Zealand. She followed him there, and he wasn't particularly surprised one morning when Nancy, holding the baby and wearing her twenty-dollar goldpiece, came aboard and asked brightly:

"Well, Captain Grant, what kind of luck have thee been having?"

Because Nancy's adventures worked out so well, a number of other Nantucket women started going to sea with their husbands. And after that, "gams" between whaleships became increasingly popular.

A "gam" was a social meeting between the crews of two vessels. Often, when two Nantucket whaleships met in the Pacific and "spoke" each other, they'd sail in company for a few days, while the officers and crews swapped news from home, and exchanged information about whales and savages. Each ship would lower a whaleboat, and the officers and men would row back and forth to pay their visits.

Special gam chairs were built for the captain's wives, so that they could be lowered modestly into the whaleboats without giving too revealing a show of underwear to the oarsmen below. A gam chair was mounted in a small box, open on the top and with a door in the front. A note in one of Captain Grant's logs says that nine other captains' wives came over to his ship one Christmas, to hold a "simper"— apparently the female equivalent of a gam—with Nancy.

Instead of resenting the presence of women and children, the crews enjoyed this touch of home. A captain's wife often insisted on better food and living conditions for the hands. And his young children, who were perfect stooges for the wildest kind of sea stories that the forecastle men delighted in telling, helped to break the monotony. The crew spoiled the children shamefully, and the captain's wife reciprocated by spoiling the crew—making them cookies and such dishes as raisin pudding steamed in sailcloth, and interceding when the captain tried to punish them.

For instance, Captain John Norton's wife, Charity, once came on deck and found that he had seized up in the rigging six deserters who had just been recaptured. Charity demanded indignantly to know what the captain intended to do with them.

"Lick 'em," said Captain Norton.

"No sir-ee, thee'll do no such thing," announced Charity.

Her statement proved accurate, too, because Captain Norton sheepishly had the men cut down.

Life for children aboard whaleships was instructive, but occasionally boring. Often they learned to navigate and figure foreign exchange before they learned how to spell. Usually their mothers made them do their lessons every day, and of course they picked up geography from first-hand experience.

An eight-year-old girl, Laura Jernegan Spear, kept a newsy log of her cruise on the *Roman,* commanded by her father. These excerpts give poignant insight of the every-day life aboard a whaleship, as seen through a child's eyes:

"It is Sunday and a very pleasant day. I have read 2 story books. This is my journal. Goodbye for today."

"It is a warm day. I shall finish my third reader this afternoon."

"We have 135 barrels of oil, 60 of hump back and 75 of sperm. We had 2 birds. Thare is one now. one died. There names were Dick and Lulu. Dick died and Lulu is go-ing to."

"Lulu died last night. It is quite smooth today."

"Papa made a trap and caught five mice. Mama has some hens that have laid 37 eggs."

"I went on board the *Emile Morgan* and had a nice time. Mrs. Dexter gave me some cards to play with, and a bottle of hair oil, and she gave me a little dog but we forgot him."

"Would you like to hear some news? Well I don't know any."

"We had beans for dinner. For tea we had biskit. I am getting along nicely with my lessons."

"We had pancakes for supper. They were real good. The Longitude was 117–23. I don't know what the Latitude was."

"We saw whales this morning, we lowered the boats and we got six. The men are cutting them in now."

"The men are cutting in the whales. They smell dredfully. Goodbye for today."

"There is a fly on my finger. He has flew off now. I can't think of much to write."

9. LOCAL BOY BECOMES CHIEF

A generation before whaling got so cut and dried that women and children sometimes went along for the ride, young William Cary shipped out of Nantucket aboard the *Oeno*, commanded by Captain Samuel Riddell. She crossed the Atlantic, doubled the Cape of Good Hope in "boisterous" weather, and sailed into the Pacific. Her crew had killed four whales, and she had fifty barrels of oil aboard, when she went aground and beat herself to pieces on a reef near the Fiji Islands the night of April 13, 1825. All hands abandoned ship in the whaleboats. William, who had a nice feeling for cliches and whose internal organs sometimes seem to have weighed a ton, subsequently wrote in his journal:

"It was with heavy hearts that we gazed back upon the wreck of what had so lately been our home."

Land—Turtle Island—was about nine miles away, and they rowed for it with fear making their "stummicks" feel like lead. And they had good cause for fear because, as every whaleman knew in 1825, of all the cannibals who inhabited the Pacific, the Fiji Islanders were the fiercest and the hungriest.

On the Fijis, life was held so cheaply that when a chief built a house, he buried a slave alive, for good luck, in each foundation posthole. And when he launched a big war canoe, he tied living men between two logs—like the rungs of a horizontal ladder—and slid the canoe over them. Their crushed bodies kept the canoe from being damaged by the coral.

Some gourmets among the cannibal chiefs made eunuchs of young men, and kept them in pens until they were fat enough for a tender feast. To lord their high stations and prosperity over their subjects, the chiefs often carried a spare foot tied around their necks, and made a big production of indulging in between-meal snacks. Fijians ate their friends and relatives, as well as their enemies, and the biggest insult you could hurl at a man was, "Boy, I'll roast you to a crisp."

When the *Oeno* crew landed on Turtle Island, the Fiji natives who lined the shore seemed fairly friendly. Captain Riddell took out his pocket watch and urged the chief to listen to the tick-tock. The chief did so, and "started back with fright and astonishment," William reported. Then the captain gave the chief the watch as a present, and all seemed well.

How did William react when he saw his first undressed woman? Well, to hear him tell it, there was no reaction at all. In fact one apparently is meant to gather that whereas William may have been an object of considerable curiosity to the women, he gave them no more than a cursory glance.

"Some women came down to the landing, looked at us, and returned to the town," he wrote. Then, quickly changing the subject and decently diverting his eyes and attention to the males, he added:

"The men were large and well formed, of a dark color, some almost black. Their only covering was a strip of matting made from the bark of a tree, twisted and wound several times around their bodies."

As a sort of postscript, he concluded his description of the natives with the brief notation that, "The women wore about their waist a similar covering."

The natives gave the white men some food and led them to a village, where they were assigned two huts. All went well at first. The Fiji men "came and spent the evenings with us, sang a song or two, and evidently employed all their arts and powers of pleasing to reconcile us to our condition."

But after a couple of weeks, some natives from the atoll of Omo came to visit on Turtle Island, and they were a good deal less friendly than the hosts.

One of the visitors strode into the Nantucketers' hut and boldly tried to help himself to some of their clothing. A crew member grabbed the clothes away from the savage and kicked him so solidly in the naked rear that he was propelled through what passed for the door.

"This treatment he did not relish," William wrote. "He took his club and beat the ground most furiously, and expressed his displeasure by every possible gesture."

Captain Riddell begged his men to be friendly at all costs, and to let the natives take whatever they wanted.

"Well it would have been," William records darkly in the inverted writing style subsequently made famous by *Time* Magazine, "if the crew had heeded the advice of our worthy captain."

But Nantucketers were not accustomed to being pushed around, least of all by heathen savages. A few hours later, when the crew was eating some roasted yams, a native entered the hut and insultingly reached into the serving bowl to help himself.

"One of our crew rapped his knuckles, telling him to keep his black paws out of the victuals," said William. "This so enraged him that he, too, got his club and beat the ground."

Two days later, while William was out exploring on a nearby hill, he heard a "great shout in the valley below"— and every member of the *Oeno* crew except him was massacred. William spares us the gory details.

The Nantucket boy hid in a cave for several days, but finally thirst and hunger drove him down to the beach to look for water and shellfish. He was almost immediately discovered by two savages, one armed with a boat hatchet and the other with a knife. They came rushing at him.

"I sat down in the path with my back toward them, expecting to have the hatchet driven into my head, and not wishing to see the blow," William wrote.

But for some reason, instead of killing the boy, the two savages spoke to him in friendly tones and led him back to the village. There he was fed and made comfortable, and a kindly old chief invited him to become his son and move into his hut. William quickly and thankfully accepted.

Meanwhile, the natives were having a wonderful time with all the stores, muskets, knives, and watches they had seized from the *Oeno* men and from the ship herself, before she broke up on the coral reef. They didn't know how to fire the guns, but they aimed them and hollered "bang," and then clutched their own "stummicks" as if they had been shot and toppled over to "die" in dramatic, gurgling convulsions.

But after a couple of weeks, word was received that another group of savages, from Lahcameber Island, planned to visit Turtle Island. This news threw the Turtle men into alarm, and they quickly gathered together all the loot from the *Oeno* and buried it for safe-keeping.

William was alarmed, too. And as it turned out, he had reason to be. When the visitors arrived, one minor chief leaped out of his canoe, saw the white boy, and grabbed him by the arm. Another minor chief, seeing William at about the same time, grabbed him by the other arm. Then the two chiefs had a fight, with the boy still in the middle, as to who would own him.

But a major chief named Toka quickly settled the matter as soon as he stepped out of his canoe. He said that, to avoid dissension among his lieutenants, *he* would own William.

Toka was a "very amiable man," and managed to let the Nantucket boy know that if any of his men tried to harm William he "would correct them." Deciding on which side his bread was buttered, William told Toka that the Turtle

Islanders had buried the loot from the *Oeno*, in order to hide it from the invaders. Toka and his men then "commenced abusing the poor islanders shamefully, and made them bring forward all the plunder they had got from the ship."

When the invaders left Turtle Island, Toka took William with him, and from that point on William went native. He dressed himself in a bark breech-clout, and helped Toka and his men collect tribute from various atolls, for their king on Lahcameber Island. Although William got a terrible sunburn, he was tanned and feeling fine about a month later, when he, Toka, and the raiding party finally arrived at Lahcameber with their canoes loaded with loot. They were received with great joy there, and natives of both sexes crowded around William as Toka led him a half-mile to the palace, to introduce him to the king.

William knew that his life depended on whether the king wanted to befriend him or to eat him. So he was on his best manners. The king studied him for awhile, listened to a report from Toka, nodded, and then handed William a coconut shell full of "carver."

This was native hooch, made from a root. Various underlings chew the root and spit it into a wooden bowl, where they knead it with their hands, add water, allow it to mellow, and then strain it through coconut bark.

William swallowed the carver, and found that it wasn't bad at all. However, obviously for the benefit of his Quaker readers, he explained in his journal that, "As I look back, it makes my 'stummick' turn to think of it."

Having passed the carver test, William was asked by

the king whether he could clean the muskets from the *Oeno,* which had become badly rusted. The boy did so, and the king then ordered him to fire them.

"I shot them several times, loading and firing as fast as I could, which frightened them very much," he wrote. "They all fell at every discharge, as though they had been shot."

The king, highly satisfied, said that William would live with him as his son. The king was surrounded by numerous wives, as well as by six other female attendants, and His Majesty ordered them to feed their new prince.

"I at first objected to being fed," William reported, "but the king insisted on my conforming to his rules as I was his son and ought to do just as he did."

That's just about the only mention that William made about native wives and attendants. But one can read between the lines. The king was surrounded by women. The king's son was supposed to behave just as the king did.

"Rather than displease him," William added piously, "I submitted."

William wrote little about cannibalism, except to note that it was commonplace. Perhaps this was another subject on which he figured that, insofar as his standing back at Nantucket was concerned, the less said the better.

At any rate, he lived with the king for about a year, and then went off on another tribute-gathering party. While on the island of Motosick, he was astounded one day to see a canoe land, and a white man step out of it, along with a score of natives. The white man walked up to William, extended his hand, and said, "Hullo, William Cary. Don't you know David Whippey?"

"Yes," William replied, "I formerly knew him. He was a townsman of mine, and an old playmate."

"Well I am that David Whippey."

William wrote that he was "dumb with astonishment," and that his "joy was unbounded."

David had come to the Fijis aboard the brig *Calder,* and said he had been sent ashore thirteen months before to trade for turtle shells. Either his ship had left him or he had decided to desert. At any rate, he had become a chief, was held in high regard, and was free to travel anywhere in the islands.

The two Nantucket boys joined forces and became favorites with all the powerful kings and chiefs. With their muskets, the two were worth hundreds of savages in raids on enemy tribes.

During one such raid, on the village of Angarmy, William barely escaped being wounded and possibly killed by a shower of arrows. But at the sound of rifle fire, the villagers became so terrified that they tried to buy off the attackers by offering them all of their whales' teeth and their chief's daughter—whales' teeth and women being the accepted form of currency.

But William's party stormed the village anyway, killed forty warriors including one who was hiding in the top of a coconut tree, and captured much legal tender in the form of women.

In an infrequent reference to cannibalism, William conceded in his journal that the forty dead men were carried back home and "divided among each tribe."

On one other occasion, William made a long journey to attend the funeral of a king who had been especially kind to him, and who had been assassinated by a brother in the Fiji equivalent of a palace murder.

William wrote that the dead king's face was painted black, which must have been a case of gilding the lily, and that he was decked out "as though prepared for war."

The king's wives sat around him and mournfully chanted, "Waloa nungu turang owsar cani lolocoo," which when freely translated means, "Oh, my dear king, we will follow you soon." They were certainly oh-so-right about that, for within a few minutes a piece of cloth, twisted up hard, was placed around the neck of each wife, and a man was assigned to each end of the cloth. At a given signal, the men jerked the cloth. After the women were dead, they were buried with their husband. Then, as a mark of respect to the late lamented, everyone in the village shaved his head, and all the children had their little fingers cut off.

William stayed for eight more years in the Fijis, and became such a big chief that, when tribute was collected and brought in, he had the choice of selecting whatever he wanted in the way of gifts or legal tender.

During those eight years, trading ships began arriving at the Fijis, and William and David served as interpreters. Both men thus had several opportunities to return home, but they preferred to remain where they were. William wrote the *Oeno's* owner about the ship's loss and the subsequent massacre. The letter arrived at Nantucket in 1830, six years after the vessel had sailed, and a number of women put on mourning and stopped searching the horizons anxiously from the walks (the early Nantucketers *never* called them "widows' walks") on their roofs.

William doesn't make it entirely clear why he finally

decided to come home. He does say, though, that after his letter arrived at Nantucket, he himself finally got some mail from home.

David Whippey elected to stay in the Fijis, where today he has many proud and dusky descendants. But William took a ship to Sydney, and after working there for awhile, signed on as a hand aboard the ship *Tybee,* out of Salem, Massachusetts. The *Tybee* sailed around Cape Horn, and arrived off Cape Cod light October 26, 1833. After the ship anchored in Salem, William took the stage to Boston and engaged passage for Nantucket.

"After a few days, I arrived at Nantucket after an absence of nine years," he concluded his narrative. "I was received with much joy by my friends and relatives and I believe heartily welcomed by all the inhabitants."

It's too bad there isn't some more material about William's later years. Did he marry? Did he go to sea again? What did he mean when he said he *believed* he was heartily welcomed? After all, we have only his own story about how the *Oeno* was lost and how the crew was massacred. Could something have happened during that massacre which gave William a guilty conscience and thus caused him to imagine that there were reservations in the way he was welcomed home?

Probably not. In fact, almost certainly not. But it is interesting, just the same, to read William's narrative in the light of another and unrelated story of a Nantucket ship. On that ship, the *Globe,* one of the crew members actually *planned* cold-bloodedly to be the only survivor of a mutiny. At least, that's what the records seem to indicate.

10. BLOODY SAM, MUTINEER

The *Globe* had a young crew, but she wasn't a happy
ship. She sailed out of Nantucket December 20, 1822, in
command of Thomas Worth, a hard captain but a fair one.
The oldest man aboard other than the captain was the First
Mate, William Beetle, and he was only twenty-six.

As the *Globe* sailed south toward Cape Horn, Worth
did his best to make whalemen out of his inexperienced
youngsters. Whenever the weather was calm, he'd order
the whaleboats lowered and teach his crew to use the
oars. He kept four lookouts aloft most of the time, so that
they'd get the feel of being up in the mastheads, and he
kept the decks holystoned white.

The *Globe* doubled the Horn without incident and
headed into the Pacific. But there were grumblings of dis-
content about the food, the work, and Captain Worth's

discipline. The ringleader was a twenty-three-year-old Nantucket harpooner named Samuel Comstock. Comstock had been to sea ever since he was fourteen, and although he was supposed to be one of the best harpooners in the business he had an unsavory reputation on Nantucket. He was a strong, handsome man, a trouble-maker, and a natural leader. Back home on Nantucket, the girls were crazy about him—and perhaps it was that which had earned him his bad reputation. Quakers mistrusted ladies' men.

Among the members of the crew was Sam Comstock's brother, George, who was fifteen years old and who later wrote a journal about the bloody happenings aboard the *Globe*. George was on his first voyage. Reading between the lines of his journal, it is apparent that he thought his older brother may have sailed aboard the *Globe* with the deliberate intention of leading a mutiny. For one thing, Sam brought along an assortment of vegetable seeds, hidden in the bottom of his sea chest. What was a harpooner doing with vegetable seeds, unless he intended to settle on some Pacific Island?

Captain Worth's harsh discipline, combined with the tension deliberately created by Sam, caused six of the *Globe*'s young crewmen to desert at Oahu, in the Sandwich (now Hawaiian) Islands. Captain Worth was forced to replace them with the only men he could find—six filthy, surly beachcombers, who had probably been kicked off other vessels because of malingering or trouble-making. The new men either signed on voluntarily or were shanghaied, and the *Globe* headed southwest in search of whales.

The six men quickly came under Sam's influence, and before long insubordination and insolence became commonplace aboard the *Globe*.

Sam fancied himself as a wrestler, and also was a master at knowing just how far he could go, within his rights, toward defying the authority of the officers. Deciding it would serve his purpose to humiliate one of the officers, he challenged the third mate, Nathaniel Fisher, to a wrestling match. Since Sam was careful to deliver the challenge with a smile and to couch it in sporting terms, Fisher couldn't interpret it as a threat of violence.

Somewhat to Sam's surprise, the third mate quickly accepted the challenge. For one thing, Mr. Fisher had been itching to get his hands on the insolent harpooner. And for another, although the third mate was some twenty pounds lighter than Sam, he was a skilled wrestler.

While all hands gathered to watch, Fisher and Comstock laughingly removed their shirts. Everyone knew, though, that the laughter was a pose and that the match amounted to a test of authority between the officers and the crew.

With Captain Worth acting as referee, the two men squared off. Sam went into a wrestler's half crouch, circling warily around Mr. Fisher, who stood poised and erect on the balls of his feet. Sam wasn't smiling any more. While the crew urged him on, he found what he thought was an opening and rushed with head down at the third mate. But Fisher sidestepped nimbly, and applied a jerking, twisting headlock which decked Sam with a humiliating thud. The harpooner was momentarily stunned and couldn't resist as Fisher pinned his shoulders to the deck.

"Good work, Mr. Fisher," announced Captain Worth.

The whole affair was over in a matter of seconds, and Fisher had disposed of Sam with such ease that the officers—and even some crew memebers—couldn't help but chuckle. Fisher started to put on his shirt.

Half-dazed, Sam got to his feet. As his head cleared and he heard the mocking laughter, his face flushed and he punched the third mate in blind hate. The blow caught Fisher by surprise. Of course, striking an officer was an extremely serious offense. But Fisher preferred to interpret the blow as part of the wrestling match, so he picked Sam up again and bounced him three times, as hard as he could, on the deck. All the wind and fight went out of Comstock, then, and he had to be carried to his bunk by a couple of his friends. His brother wrote that Sam swore he was fouled, and "vowed vengeance" against Fisher.

After Sam's licking, some members of the crew became more insolent than ever. Matters reached a head as the ship neared the equator, when one of the hands, Joe Thomas, failed to show up when he was called for his watch. By then, it was apparent to everyone that some of the hands were trying to see just how much they could get away with, before Captain Worth yanked them into line.

Thomas, a filthy-tongued, dirty little man, was one of the six who had been taken aboard at Oahu. His absence on deck caused Captain Worth to see red.

"Go below and tell Thomas to lay up here on the double," Worth ordered Sam Comstock.

Sam did as he was told, but returned in a few minutes without the seaman.

"Where's Thomas?" demanded the Captain.

"He says he's busy, sir," smirked Sam. "He says he'll be up in a few minutes."

Mr. Worth, who had a fairly low boiling point, was furious. He turned to Third Mate Fisher.

"Please go below, Mr. Fisher," he grated, "and *bring* me Thomas."

Fisher disappeared into the forecastle, and the men on deck could hear him roar. Within a matter of seconds, Thomas emerged, with Fisher behind him. But even so, Thomas slouched slowly up to the captain, as if daring anyone to make him move faster. All hands were watching to see if the little malingerer would get away with this latest bit of insolence.

Captain Worth, with arms akimbo and head thrust forward, waited on his quarterdeck for Thomas to arrive.

When the seaman finally stood in front of him, Worth asked with deceptive calm:

"Why didn't thee come topside when thee were called?"

"I hadn't finished eating my breakfast, Captain," Thomas grinned.

Of course, everyone knew that when a sailor was summoned to duty, he responded immediately—whether he had finished his breakfast or whether he had had no breakfast at all.

"I've a mind to give thee a breakfast thee won't forget," threatened Worth.

"If you do, you'll pay for it," said Thomas, in a threat which almost amounted to mutiny.

Captain Worth turned on his heel, and addressed First Mate Beetle.

"Seize that man up, Mr. Beetle," the Captain ordered. "I want him to have twenty-five licks. Call all hands, and bring down the lookouts."

The Second and Third Mates, John Lumbard (or Lumbert) and Fisher, grabbed Thomas. While he kicked and screamed obscenities, they dragged him to the starboard, mainmast ratlines, and spreadeagled him there so that only his toes touched the deck. The four lookouts, on orders from Beetle, scrambled down the ratlines and joined the rest of the crew on deck.

Beetle ripped Thomas' filthy canvas shirt up the back, and tore the two halves off the seaman's shoulders. Thomas' pale skin was as filthy as the shirt. Third Mate Fisher picked up a wicked lash of knotted rope.

"All ready, Mr. Fisher?" asked Captain Worth.

Fisher, holding the lash first in one hand and then in the other, finished rolling up his sleeves. "Ready, sir."

Worth nodded. Fisher deliberately swung the heavy, three-foot lash above his head, and brought the rope whistling down on Thomas' back. The seaman gasped as if amazed that anything could cause such incredible pain, shuddered, and then screamed like a woman.

"One," said Captain Worth.

Fisher swung the rope around his head again. The lash whistled and Thomas screamed. That time, the skin popped open on his back.

"Two," said Captain Worth.

By the count of fifteen, Thomas' screams had died into whimpering moans. Fisher was sweating from his exertions, and the lash—red and sodden—spit flecks of blood every time he swung it above his head. Fisher looked inquiringly at the Captain.

"Get on with it, Mr. Fisher," nodded Worth. "Twenty-five."

The Third Mate swung—and swung again.

"Sixteen," intoned Worth. "Seventeen."

At the count of twenty-five, the swaying toes of Thomas' bare feet stirred a pool of blood on the deck, and Thomas himself was unconscious.

Sam and a couple of other men revived him with a bucket of salt water, and carried him to the forecastle. Fisher tied the lash to a painter and threw it over the side to wash it out. The lookouts scrambled back to the mast-heads.

Sam Comstock decided that his followers were now ready for mutiny. Although they knew that Thomas had deserved the flogging, they were shaken by its severity. Twenty-five licks by a strong officer like Fisher were enough to leave a man more dead than alive.

Deciding to make the most of the men's resentment, Comstock made plans to seize the ship that same night.

Either by design or coincidence, Sam made his move while his young brother, George, had the trick at the helm. George didn't take part in the mutiny and he was explicit about what happened.

George said that a few minutes before midnight, he picked up the helmsman's rattle from the binnacle to summon the new watch. George was about to shake the rattle, when Sam appeared silently out of the darkness. Sam was carrying a boarding knife, and his face was twisted with hate.

"Put it down," Sam whispered, pointing toward the rattle with the knife. "If you make a sound, I'll send you to hell."

George put down the rattle.

"If you want to live," said Sam, "hold her full and steady."

Three of the men who had been picked up at Oahu—Silas Payne, John Oliver, and William Humphries—joined Sam. Humphries, a Negro, had a lantern, which he lit from the light at the binnacle. Sam traded his boarding knife for a broad axe that Payne was carrying. The four crept stealthily toward the officers' quarters.

There were three cabins for the officers, all of which opened into their central mess hall. Captain Worth and First Mate Beetle each had a cabin of his own, and the other two mates shared the third room.

Sam pushed open the door of Worth's cabin and swung the axe twice at the sleeping Captain, practically severing his head. The captain gushed a fountain of blood which saturated Sam's clothing, and the harpooner was a frightening sight as he backed out of the door and turned to enter the cabin of Beetle.

Silas Payne, a burly sadist, was supposed to have killed Beetle with the boarding knife. But the first mate, awaking just as Payne stabbed at him, managed to roll in time to escape with no more than a flesh wound. As Sam entered, he dived at Beetle and wrestled him to the floor, where Payne stabbed him again. Sam then broke loose, picked up the axe, and brought it down on Beetle's chest.

When Sam emerged from Beetle's cabin, his hair and face—as well as his clothes—were dripping blood. He was such a gory sight that Humphries took one look at him, gasped, and dropped the lantern. The flame went out, and Sam cursed the Negro.

Feeling in the dark, Sam found the door of the cabin shared by Second Mate Lumbard and Third Mate Fisher. But the mutineers had made so much noise that they had tipped their hand, and Lumbard and Fisher had locked and barricaded the door.

Cursing some more, Sam left his three fellow mutineers on guard and returned to the binnacle to re-light the lamp Humphries had dropped.

Young George, who was sobbing silently in terror, wrote that he had never seen a more frightening sight than his blood-drenched brother.

"What are you crying about?" Sam asked.

"I am afraid that they will hurt me," George recorded that he replied.

"I will hurt you myself if you talk in that manner."

Carrying the lighted lantern, Sam went back to the officers' quarters, loaded two muskets that he found there, affixed bayonets to them, and fired the lock off the door.

"Did that shot hit either of you?" Sam called through the door.

Fisher said the shot had hit him in the mouth.

"Are you going to kill us, Comstock?" Lumbard shouted.

"Oh no, I guess not," Sam called back carelessly.

With that, the harpooner kicked open the door and rushed into the room, intending to bayonet Fisher. But even with a bullet in his mouth, the third mate was more than a match for Sam. Jumping aside, Fisher slapped Sam and grabbed the musket out of his hands. Quickly, then, the third mate aimed the bayonet point at Sam's heart, and backed him up against a bulkhead. The other three mutineers kept their distance.

"The whole crew is behind me to a man," Sam lied desperately. "If you kill me, they'll fry both you and Lumbard in the try works. If you give me back that musket, I'll promise that no harm comes to you."

Trustingly Fisher gave Sam back the musket. Then while Payne covered Fisher with a gun, Sam turned and ran the bayonet through Lumbard, an inoffensive man and the father of six children. Lumbard fell to the floor, and Sam savagely bayoneted him twice more.

"I should have known better," sighed Third Mate Fisher. "If there is no hope, I will at least die like a man." He turned his back to Comstock, and said calmly, "I am ready."

Sam pointed a musket at the back of Fisher's head, and fired. Stepping over the bodies, he emerged on deck, shook his fist, and roared:

"I'm a bloody man. I'm a *bloody* man, and I have a bloody hand."

There wasn't any doubt about that!

The only one of the mutineers who had actually helped Sam with the killing was Silas Payne, so Sam named Payne his first mate. Payne summoned all hands, and had the bodies of the four officers brought on deck. One by one, the bodies were pitched unceremoniously over the side. But when it came time to pitch Lumbard's body, the second mate was found to be alive and conscious, despite his three bayonet wounds.

Lumbard clutched the rail and pleaded for his life.

"Comstock, I have never harmed thee," he began, "and . . ."

Sam stepped on his fingers, and the second mate sighed and let go.

The blood was scrubbed up, and rum and extra rations broken out. "Captain" Comstock ordered all whaling equipment—except one try-pot—to be thrown over the side.

He kept this try-pot for reasons of morale, which became apparent when he made all members of the crew sign an oath saying they would fight along side of him. Sam rather relished the idea, which he had first expressed to Mr. Fisher, of boiling people in oil. The oath stated that the penalty for refusing to fight was death and, "The manner of their death is this: They shall be bound hand and foot, and boiled in the try-pot of boiling oil."

Sam needed a scapegoat, to show the crew that he demanded complete loyalty. A few days after the mutiny, the scapegoat emerged in the form of Humphries, who was observed loading a pistol. Sam immediately accused the Negro of plotting a new mutiny.

A court martial was convened on the spot, and Humphries was quickly found guilty. For some reason, it was decided at the last minute to hang the Negro from a boom rigged over the side, instead of boiling him in oil.

A noose was slipped over Humphries' head, and the line was run through an overhead block. So that everyone would share responsibility for the execution, Comstock ordered all hands to stand by to hoist away.

"You have fourteen seconds to live," Sam told the Negro. "If you have anything to say, say it."

Bewildered by the speed of his "trial" and the forth-coming execution, Humphries swallowed and began, "Little did I think I was born to come to this . . ."

Comstock gave the signal, and the men hoisted. Lifted clear of the deck, poor Humphries dangled over the side, suspended from the boom. After they were sure he was dead, Comstock cut the rope and the body splashed into the sea.

That made a total of five deaths for which Sam was responsible. If his master plan was to be the lone survivor of the *Globe*, he was off to a good start. Certainly Sam knew he could never safely go home again, as long as a single one of his shipmates was alive. So the young "captain" began looking for an island where there was plenty of good vegetation and fresh water, and where the natives would be amenable to his rule.

As Sam sailed the *Globe* through the Marshalls and Gilberts, occasionally going ashore with well-armed exploring parties, life became a series of wild and drunken debauches. "First Mate" Payne twice shot native men while he was ashore, simply for the pleasure of watching them die. And Payne was so rough on the women brought back to the ship by exploring parties that even Sam felt sorry for them. If a girl resisted Payne's crude advances, he often would punch her full in the mouth, and then giggle as blood trickled down her chin.

Girls he dragged into his cabin were sometimes so badly beaten that, when he finally passed out in a drunken stupor, they emerged whimpering on deck, crawling on their hands and knees.

Some of the groups of girls came aboard without urging,

and some were brought aboard at sword point. They were drunkenly fought over and abused. Often, when the crew got tired of them, the girls were pushed over the side to swim ashore if they could, while the crew hove anchor and sailed the *Globe* away.

After a month or two of sailing, exploring, and debauching, Sam at last decided he had found the sort of island he wanted. It was an atoll called Mille in the Mulgraves, Marshall group, 380 miles southeast of Kwajalein and 3000 miles north of New Zealand. The Micronesian natives there seemed friendly. Sam warned his crew, especially "First Mate" Payne, that on this particular island there were to be no shootings of native men just for the sport of it, and—at least for the time being—discretion in the manner of raping women.

Comstock anchored the *Globe* in a lagoon close to the beach, and his men were on their best behavior as they began ferrying supplies ashore. The natives obligingly lent a hand, and Sam rewarded them with handsome presents of clothes, food, and weapons.

This largesse of Comstock's part continued for three or four days, while the crew was building a small camp in a clump of coconut trees near the beach. Payne soon became irritated and suspicious at the way Sam was currying favor with the natives and demanded to know exactly why the "captain" was arming the natives. A fierce argument ensued, in a tent that Payne had built on the beach. The argument almost certainly would have come to blows, except for the fact that Sam suddenly ended his bluster and put on an act of injured feelings.

Sam said that since his leadership was questioned and

since no one seemed to appreciate all the risks he had run, he didn't see why he should devote any more time and effort to the welfare of the crew. Sam added that as far as he was concerned, Payne could have the thankless job of being the boss. As for Sam, he said he was washing his hands of the whole affair, and from then on intended to shift for himself.

Before Payne could object, Sam stalked out of the tent and disappeared in the direction of the native village.

Thereafter, for the next couple of days, Sam was seen occasionally at a distance, leading fairly large groups of native warriors on walks over the atoll. Some of the natives carried muskets, which Sam had given them earlier. Occasionally, sounds of gunfire were heard from the interior of the island. Correctly or not, Payne decided that Comstock was training the natives for an assault on the camp. Consequently, Payne quickly had his men dig trenches around the camp, and posted armed sentries in the underbrush.

On the morning of the third day, Sam approached the camp at the head of a column of natives. Comstock couldn't have been planning to attack at that time, because the natives were unarmed. He was smiling and he walked jauntily as if he and the natives had come for a friendly gam.

But Payne didn't trust him, and shouted orders for the sentries to be on guard. Sam saw the sentries rise from the underbrush and draw a bead on him.

He rushed forward, then, shouting, "Don't shoot me. Don't shoot me. I won't hurt you."

"Fire," roared Payne. "It's a trick. Fire."

The sentries obeyed. Sam stumbled, ran a few feet more,

and then toppled over onto his face in the sand. His natives turned about and fled. And Payne, picking up an axe, walked deliberately to the writhing body and cut off Sam's head—a bloody end for the bloody man.

Later that day, they sewed up Sam's head and body in canvas, and buried him on the beach. Gilbert Smith, a Nantucket Quaker boy, read a chapter from the Bible over the grave, and Sam's brother George "wept unashamed."

Aside from Sam Comstock, no Nantucketers had participated in the mutiny. Consequently, Payne kept a close watch on them and on the *Globe* herself, to make sure they wouldn't try to steal the ship and escape. Since no seaman, however able, could navigate a ship without a compass, Payne thought that he wouldn't have to worry about their taking the *Globe* if he secured her compasses.

Payne seems to have been somewhat of a psychologist. In order to indicate to the Nantucketers that he knew what was going on in their minds, he ordered three of them—George Comstock, Gilbert Smith, and Peter Kidder —to row out to the *Globe* and bring him the two compasses from the binnacle.

Since Payne was a forecastle hand and not an officer, it was understandable that he made the mistake of forgetting there was a *third* compass on almost every whaleship—the compass that hung suspended over the bunk of the captain and enabled him to tell, even in the middle of the night, whether the helmsman was on course.

Comstock, Smith, and Kidder were forecastle hands, too. But Nantucket seamen were an entirely different breed from such rough adventurers as Payne. It was practically taken for granted that every Nantucket boy would someday be a whaling captain—like his father, his uncles, and his cousins. Nantucketers actually were being trained as captains, from the day they first shipped as cabin boys.

So Comstock, Smith and Kidder didn't forget about the compass in the captain's cabin. Once they got aboard the *Globe,* they held a brief conference and decided to try to take the ship that night. It was vital to their plans that a compass remain at the helm. Counting on the fact that Payne wasn't a very observant sailor, they made up their minds to risk the gamble of bringing him the captain's compass and only one compass from the binnacle. The second binnacle compass was left in place, by the wheel.

Luckily, Payne gave the instruments no more than a cursory glance, when they were deposited in his tent. And that night, confident no one would be foolhardy enough to steal a ship without a compass, he relaxed his watch over the Nantucketers.

The three had found it impossible to tell their plans to all the Nantucketers, because Payne had broken up the camp into several groups and it would have aroused suspicion to go from one group to another. Altogether, there were only six men who swam silently out to the *Globe* that night, and climbed aboard.

Once the six were on deck, silence was abandoned for speed. Four men went aloft to break out sails, and as the first blocks started to squeak, a lookout on the beach shouted the alarm. Payne came rushing to the shore, and quickly had a whaleboat launched. By the time the mutineers started pulling at the oars, the sails on the *Globe* could be seen blossoming from her masts in the moonlight.

Young George Comstock, at the helm of the *Globe,* put

the wheel over sharply as the first sails filled in the light breeze. The channel leading from the lagoon was narrow and tricky. Not until the vessel had steerage-way, and her anchor line came up slack, did Peter Kidder in the bow dare to cut the hawser with a broadaxe.

For a few minutes, the whaleboat continued to close the distance to the *Globe,* while Payne urged on his oarsmen. But the four men aloft had been well trained by Captain Worth, and they swiftly cracked on every available piece of canvas. As more and more sails filled, the *Globe* gradually started to pull away from her pursuers. Finally Payne realized he had lost the race, and had to content himself with firing musket balls and terrible oaths at the *Globe's* stern.

The six men, with only one compass and very limited provisions, sailed the *Globe* some seven thousand miles to Valparaiso. They arrived at the Chilean port in June, 1824, and their news of the most bloody mutiny of modern times quickly spread through the maritime world. When the word reached Nantucket, few tears were shed for Sam Comstock. The islanders, whose everyday living depended on successful voyages, were principally concerned about the possibility that the *Globe* mutiny would cause other whalemen to defy the authority of their captains. At a specially called town meeting, the citizens of Nantucket passed a resolution demanding that the United States bring Payne and his lieutenants to justice.

Carrying a copy of the resolution, a delegation of Nantucket Quakers urged President Monroe to send a warship to the Mulgraves, and make an example of the mutineers. Monroe, who was just going out of office after having served two terms, agreed it was important that the mutineers be punished as soon as possible. So he immediately ordered the U.S. Schooner *Dolphin,* captained by Lieutenant Commander John Percival, to proceed to the atoll and bring back the ringleaders, dead or alive.

Payne had flown into a rage when the *Globe* disappeared. He realized that it would only be a matter of time before the Navy started looking for him—and that the men who had sailed away in the *Globe* would tell the Navy exactly where to look.

Payne therefore decided he would have to move to some distant island. He had two whaleboats, and under his direction the men started tearing apart one boat, so that the planks could be used to increase the freeboard and build a deck on the other.

While this work was going on, Payne and his companion Oliver explored the nearby islands. And after one such trip, they returned to camp with two pretty young native girls, not more than fourteen or fifteen years old.

After one hellish night with Payne, his girl escaped and went back to her village. Payne must have felt that her running away caused him to lose face with his men. And matters weren't helped any by the fact that Oliver and *his* girl got along like two lovebirds. Arming himself with a musket and pistol, the sadistic mutineer set out to find the young runaway, and bring her back.

Although the girl had been hidden by her people, they surrendered her when Payne threatened to shoot up the village. He returned to camp with her shortly after dark, put her in irons, and dragged her into his tent. There he tied her to a post, and in the light of a whaleoil lamp he flogged her until she lost consciousness.

Because of the flogging, the natives secretly vowed vengeance. And the rest of the story parallels closely the massacre of the *Oeno* crew. The natives started stealing from the camp, and there were so many of them that the white men didn't dare to stop them. When the natives found out that the white men were afraid, they openly and insultingly helped themselves to everything in sight. After the camp was stripped bare, they deliberately humiliated the white men and made them crawl.

Then, without any warning, a wrinkled old hag whose breasts hung down to her waist like razor strops cackled, shrieked, and plunged a spear through Columbus Worth's stomach. Half a dozen whooping savages fell on Payne and hammered out his brains with jagged rocks. Two mutineers broke away and started running, but they didn't take more than a couple of steps before a cluster of spears hit their backs, and they fell forward in the sand like giant pincushions.

One by one, the crewmen were butchered. But at the very start of the slaughter, an old native couple had pounced on William Lay, a young and handsome blond boy from Connecticut, and shielded him with their bodies. Expecting death at any moment, William remained motionless under them.

When the massacre was over, the old couple picked up William, and from then on he was their son. The woman took him to her house and rubbed him with coconut oil.

The reader may begin to think that every whaleman was a budding author, but the fact is that William Lay—like George Comstock—also wrote up his experiences.

William, perhaps purposely building up a dramatic climax for his booklet, recorded that while he was being rubbed down he wept for the loss of his best friend and shipmate, Cyrus Hussey of Nantucket. Neither William nor Cyrus had taken part in the mutiny, and they alone had always been kind and friendly to the natives. What also depressed William, he wrote, was that "I should be left alone to drag out a weary existence with beings strangers to the endearing ties which bind the hearts of civilized men."

But a few hours later, a group of natives brought a white boy into the village and the boy turned out to be none other than Cyrus Hussey. Cyrus had been away from the camp when the slaughter occurred, so he too was spared. Naturally, he and William had a joyful reunion.

"The reader must pardon any attempt to describe my feelings," William choked.

The boys soon adopted native dress and, although William didn't say so, he must have made quite a hit with the native girls. His whiskers were just beginning to grow, and he raised a luxuriant blond beard, to go with his golden hair and blue eyes.

"I was often complimented on the improvement of my appearance," he conceded, "as my skin became nearly as black as their own."

Some of the girls wanted him to stretch his ears down to his shoulders, like the other men, but William drew the line at that!

Cyrus, meanwhile, was moved to a nearby island, since the natives thought there would be less chance the boys would escape if they were kept apart.

Cyrus and William lived on the Mulgraves for about two years. Then, on November 29, 1825, the ship dispatched by President Monroe sailed bravely up to Mille, and dropped anchor outside the lagoon.

The natives were terrified, partly because they didn't want to lose William, of whom they had grown very fond; but principally because they were afraid they'd be punished for having killed the rest of the *Globe* crew. So the natives made up their minds to hide William and to ambush and kill the crew of the U.S.S. *Dolphin*.

William told them that he had a better plan. He'd go down to the beach and, as a landing party from the *Dolphin* approached, he'd call to the white men and assure them that the natives were friendly. Then the whites would be completely off guard, and the ambush would be a cinch. Since the natives had come to trust William's judgment, especially in battle maneuvers, they went along with his plan.

And so as a fifteen-man landing party rowed in from the *Dolphin*, a blond, bearded youth, naked except for a belt from which two strategically located mats dangled fore and aft, stood waving on the beach. A pace or so behind him were a hundred warriors, all seemingly unarmed and all doing their best to smile a warm, hospitable greeting.

"Can you hear me?" William shouted to the boat.

"We hear you," replied Lieutenant Hiram Paulding, U.S.N., who was in charge of the landing party.

"Don't land unless you have plenty of guns. They plan to kill you. Act friendly, but be on guard."

"Right and thanks," shouted Paulding. "We're heavily armed."

"Be careful, will you? I don't want to get a spear in my back."

William then turned to the savages. "I told them you were wonderful people and wanted to give them a big feast," he translated into their tongue. "Now all nod your heads and give them a great big smile."

The savages did as William told them.

When the small boat grounded on the beach, the Americans leaped out, armed to the teeth. I suppose they were Marines. But whoever they were, they landed and had the Situation Well in Hand. William raced to them, still wondering whether he would get a spear in his back. Paulding took him by the hand and got him into the boat, while the other Americans stood guard.

The natives realized William had tricked them, but they had too much sense to charge fifteen armed men. However, the old man who had helped save William's life and who had become his father simply couldn't bear to see his blond son go away. Ignoring the muskets and the bayonets, the old savage pushed through the guards, threw his arms around William's neck and begged the boy to stay. The old man wouldn't let go until someone pointed a pistol at his ear. He sobbed as he returned to the line of no-longer-smiling warriors.

Later, after William was safely aboard the *Dolphin*, he must have felt sorry for the old couple which had adopted him. When Lieutenant Commander Percival decided to go ashore and lecture the natives on the folly of killing white people, William went along as interpreter and gave a handkerchief to his adopted father and a few beads to his adopted mother. After his lecture, the master of the *Dolphin* presented the natives with some vegetable seeds, three tomahawks, an axe, a male and a female cat, and a male and female hog. He urged them to let the animals multiply, and to eat regular pig instead of long pig.

To show their appreciation, the natives reciprocated by opening Sam Comstock's grave and making Percival a present of Sam's severed skull.

When they returned to the *Dolphin,* William directed the ship to the island where Cyrus Hussey lived. The natives there had hidden Cyrus, but they produced him when Percival threatened to kill every last one of them.

There was a happy celebration once William and Cyrus were together again aboard the naval schooner. "We will not attempt to describe," wrote William, who then went ahead and described it in some detail, "our joy on seeing the Star Spangled Banner floating once more."

So with Old Glory waving bravely in the exotic tropic breeze, the two brave lads bid a fond farewell to the islands where they had had so many spine-tingling adventures, and the *Dolphin* sailed with a white bone in her teeth back toward the good old U.S.A.

Word of their rescue preceded them. On October 28, 1826, the *Nantucket Inquirer* published a letter from the American consul at Valparaiso saying that the *Dolphin* had just arrived there, "having on board William Lay and Cyrus M. Hussey, both grown up fine young men. All the rest belonging to the *Globe* were killed by the natives."

When Cyrus finally reached Nantucket—where his house still stands near the Old Mill—there was a big celebration for him on the wharf. I suppose that the same sort of celebration was held for William, when he got back to his home in Connecticut. As for Lieutenant Commander Percival, he was commended when he reported to Washington and presented his superiors with Sam Comstock's skull, to prove that orders to bring back the chief mutineer, dead or alive, had been carried out.

11. DAD AND THE *MINNIE R.*

I know very well that I can't top the story of the *Globe* mutiny, and I have no intention of trying. I'm reminded, just the same, of the time Dad took command of the Cat-boat *Minnie R.*, after declaring her captain to be unfit for duty.

It happened in the summer of 1919, I believe, but I'm not positive of the date because unfortunately I didn't keep a journal. As part of his education program, Dad wanted to teach all of us how to sail. Eventually, he obtained a catboat of his own, called the *Rena*. But before he got the *Rena*, it was necessary for Dad himself to brush up on his limited knowledge of sailing.

Consequently he decided to combine a sailing lesson with a squantum on Coatue. He chartered the *Minnie R.* and her captain to take us to Coatue. The captain of the

165

Minnie R. also was hired to provide the food and do the cooking for the squantum, which was to be in the form of an old-fashioned New England clam and lobsterbake.

Nantucket's inner harbor is shaped like a horseshoe, with Nantucket town on one side and Coatue on the other. At the rounded part of the horseshoe is the summer-resort village of Wauwinet, named for the father of the Indian brave whose nickname translates freely into Lucky Boy. At Wauwinet you can swim in the chilly ocean surf or walk three hundred yards across the strand and swim in the smooth, warm waters of the harbor.

Today, it's possible to drive to Coatue along the beach, if you hire a jeep equipped with special, big tires. But in 1919, the only way to get there—unless you wanted to walk ten miles or so over soft sand—was by boat across the harbor.

For a week before our picnic, Dad lectured us on the theory of sailboating—how a forward thrust was obtained even when the wind was coming at you almost head-on; the functions of keels and centerboards; the necessity of tacking when the wind was against you. He also obtained from the Atheneum library pictures of full-rigged ships, like the old whaleships, and taught us the names of the masts and the various sails.

So that the skipper of the *Minnie R.* wouldn't have too hellish an experience with eight children climbing all over his boat, Dad stressed repeatedly that a captain was always in complete command of his craft, that his orders had to be obeyed explicitly, and that he was free to apply the "merrie rope's end" to members of the crew who didn't do exactly as he said.

The Nantucket waterfront has changed a great deal since the whaling days, when the harbor was forested with the masts of three hundred square-riggers and schooners at a time, being fitted for sea. Back in 1830, more than a thousand men had regular jobs on the wharfs and a steady stream of supplies came rumbling over the cobblestones in big drays. Quaker men in their homespun suits and square-toed shoes worked alongside blanket-wearing Pacific Ocean savages with their teeth filed into points, escaped or freed slaves from the South, Portuguese seamen with crimson silk sashes and brass earings. A shipyard on Brant Point bustled with activity. The rope walks, sail lofts, cooper shops, sperm-candle factories, and whale-oil refineries operated from dawn until curfew.

The five big wharfs, which used to serve the town, rotted and collapsed when whaling died. Subsequently they were rebuilt, though, to take care of small sail boats, rich men's yachts, a few fishing smacks, and of course the steamer from New Bedford. Some of the arty members of the summer colony have little studios built on the wharfs —with such names as Bide-a-wee and The Crow's Nest— where they can sketch the sailboats. Of course the artists would rather sketch quaint-looking fishing schooners, but they are few and far between. When such a schooner *does* come to Nantucket, the artists converge by the score, not only from the studios on the docks but even from such distant settlements as Wauwinet and 'Sconset. Whenever you see anyone in a beret and smock, hurrying with glassy-eyed intensity toward the docks, you can be pretty sure that a dirty little fishing schooner has come in.

The *Minnie R.* was kept at a mooring off the Straight

Wharf, originally built in 1723, and her captain had her berthed alongside the wharf. Mother had sensibly begged off from the squantum, electing to remain home with the newest baby, whom Dad always referred to proudly as the "latest model." So Dad and eight of us walked out to the wharf and prepared to get aboard.

Nantucket catboats, skippered by white-haired codgers in the summer-visitor trade, are ageless, fat, lethargic, sedate, and reliable. If the sporty sloops and multi-colored Rainbow Fleet of the Yacht Club are the highstrung race horses of the harbor, the stubby-masted catboats are the old gray mares.

The *Minnie R.* must have been forty years old in 1919, and she's still in business today and looks just about the same as she did then. In a full gale, she might suddenly come to life, tip jauntily at a five-degree angle, and get the lead out of her stern to make five or six knots. But, ordinarily she drifts along complacently, at an upright and unhurried knot or two. About the best that can be said for catboats such as the *Minnie R.* is that they get you there and they bring you back. A skipper charges his passengers by the hour, instead of by the mile, so it makes little difference to him that the "there" where his catboat takes you isn't very far. Also, since a good portion of his business comes from nice old ladies who have adventurously donned wide-brimmed canvas hats and sneakers for what they invariably describe as "a cruise on the bounding main," it suits him to bring them back safe, bone-dry, and comparatively unseasick. If one of those artists who have studios on the wharves would sketch a catboat bearing an ecstatic cargo of retired school teachers, holding parasols in one hand while trailing the other over the leeward rail in the water, I might even buy the picture myself.

The skipper of the *Minnie R.* was Cap'n Tim Adams, a native of Edgartown, Martha's Vineyard, who had had the good judgment to move to Nantucket as a boy. Cap'n Tim suffered from rheumatism, and had a tobacco-stained mustache. Like a lot of old people, he could stand almost anything except being helped at his job. He considered any offer to help to be an insulting implication that he was getting too ancient to do the work he always had done.

Aside from his tobacco-stained mustache, the most conspicuous feature of Cap'n Tim's face was his nose, which was bulbous and crisscrossed with purple veins that formed a topography of miniature mountain ridges. Although his cheeks and forehead were burned brown, his nose persisted in peeling, and stood out like an oxblood saddle on a tan shoe.

"You didn't tell me about the live bait," he complained to Dad as soon as he saw us. "You said there'd be you and eight other people."

"And here I am," Dad said loftily, "and here are the eight other people. Children are people, aren't they?"

"I ain't never been convinced of that," grumbled Cap'n Tim. "But the fire's going over on Coatue and I've already paid for the clams and lobsters, so it's too late to back out. Git aboard, then."

"What makes his nose so red?" one of my young brothers whispered to me. "And why doesn't he like us?"

"If you're going to talk like that," stormed Cap'n Tim, who had incredibly sharp ears, "we ain't going. To hell with the clams and lobsters and the fire I spent all morning making."

"What did he say?" Dad asked the captain.

"Never you mind what he said," replied Tim.

As often happened when our family went anyplace en masse, a small crowd was beginning to collect. The captain wanted to get out of there before any of his colleagues on the dock heard any further remarks about his nose.

"What did you say?" Dad sternly asked the brother. "Do you want the captain to give you the merrie rope's end?"

"If he tells you out loud," the captain roared, "I'll give *you* the merrie rope's end."

"Aye-aye, captain," grinned Dad. "Let's go then. Get aboard, live bait."

We climbed onto the *Minnie R.*, and Dad removed from his shoulders the next-to-latest model—the 1917 number. Dad had taught us the names of the two halyards and of the various parts of the ship, and the importance that good skippers place on having lines coiled and shipshape. We asked Cap'n Tim whether he wanted us to hoist the throat and the peak for him, and cast off the painter, and lower the centerboard. It turned out that he didn't.

"Don't any of you little unprintables touch a single censored thing," he hollered, interrupting our offers of assistance.

"I presume likely they could handle that mud-skow better than some Vineyard landlubbers I know," an old Nantucketer on the wharf observed loudly to a neighbor. "What would you say that sort of tassel is on end of the centerboard rope, Abe?"

"That ain't no tassel," replied Abe, equally loud. "Man, don't you know a Martha's Vineyard splice when you see one?"

Everyone on the dock laughed, and I began to feel a little sorry for Cap'n Tim.

"Would you like me to make a real neat splice for you there, Cap'n?" I asked sincerely. "My father showed me how to do it."

"No, dammit, no," shouted Tim.

"I wisht, boy, that you'd git your father to show Tim how to do it," observed Abe. "It's splices like that which git a bad name for all Nantucket captains."

Tim chose to ignore that last remark, and instead mumbled something to Dad about needing some rheumatism medicine. He disappeared for a moment into the little cabin of the *Minnie R.* and when he emerged again he seemed a little bit more cheerful. With surprising agility for a man his age, he quickly hoisted the sail, cast off, ducked under the boom and scooted aft to take the wheel.

"I've seen Army blankets that set better than that sail, ain't you, Abe?" was the parting shot of the old Nantucketer on the wharf.

"Some Vineyard lobsters that pass themselves off as sailors," agreed Abe, "ain't good enough to take in slack."

For some reason, no Nantucketer or Vineyarder likes to be called a lobster. And a man who can't be counted upon to take in slack is considered to be the worst kind of lazybones. Although Tim studied the little wind pennant on his masthead and made believe he hadn't heard these final insults, you could tell he was mad and that he put the blame on us.

The trip to Coatue took a couple of hours. Tim wouldn't let us steer or even hold the sheet, but to get us out of his hair he finally allowed us to make the *Minnie R.* shipshape. With a little help from Dad, I put a new crown splice on the centerboard rope. Dad himself, to show us how it was done, whipped the end of the painter with marline, so that it wouldn't fray any more; untied the sloppy two-half-hitches with which the painter was fastened to the mast; and retied the rope with a proper bowline. The older girls pumped out the bilge and swabbed the decks. And the younger boys coiled the halyards and tightened the turn-buckles on the sidestays.

The *Minnie R.* wasn't a mess by any means when we set out on the trip. But there was no denying that she was mighty shipshape by the time we approached Coatue. Instead of appreciating our efforts, though, Cap'n Tim kept mumbling about how he hated to have live bait and busy-bodied fat men aboard. He made three more trips to the cabin for rheumatism medicine—and each time he left the wheel he secured it, rather than give us the satisfaction of letting us hold it for him.

He also made quite a point of counting his passengers, to see if any had fallen overboard. He did this counting more or less to himself, but obviously for our benefit.

"Let's see, there's the fat father, that's one," he'd mumble, "and them three freckled girls, that's four, and . . ." The rest of the mumble would be lost in his mustache until he came to the end of the calculation, when he'd sigh with feigned disappointment:

". . . making a grand total of nine, just what we started with. Oh, well!"

The stretch of beach at Coatue that Tim had selected for the squantum drops off quite sharply, so he was able to run the bow of the *Minnie R.* almost to the shore. We jumped over the side and waded in, securing the anchor for him on the beach with enough slack so that the boat wouldn't be grounded at low tide. Tim was the last to come ashore, and before disembarking he went below for still another dose of rheumatism medicine. It must have been a big dose, because when he finally joined us on the beach—with a canvas bag of corn and seafood over his shoulder—he was positively genial.

"All right, Johnny," he told us, "if you watch close now I'll show you how to hold a real Nantucket clambake."

We had already examined a grave-like pit, about six feet long and a foot and a half deep, in which the captain had built a big fire early that morning. The bottom of the pit had been lined with a dozen rocks, each about the size of a basketball, and although the fire had burned down to embers, the rocks were still very hot.

"Now, Johnny," said our genial skipper, who had abandoned his prejudice against being helped, "all of you go down to the water and bring Cap'n Tim a pile of wet seaweed. It's got to be wet enough to put out those embers."

When the pile was collected, he covered rocks and embers with a layer of seaweed about four inches thick, which hissed and steamed immediately. The clams, lobsters and corn-on-the-cob went on top of the seaweed, and Tim then covered the food with another layer of seaweed about a foot thick. The steam smelled wonderful.

The girls went behind a sand dune and changed into their bathing suits, and the boys and Dad changed on the beach. Cap'n Tim, despite a warning from Dad that he'd better lay off the stuff, waded out to the *Minnie R.* and disappeared into the cabin again. When he came ashore, he had a decided list to starboard and there was a sizeable bulge in his hip pocket.

We swam for an hour or so, diving off the stern of the catboat, while the food steamed. Cap'n Tim probably would have objected to our getting his boat wet, if he had seen what we were up to. But he had elected to take a nap near the fire, where he was snoring gently.

After the swim, we changed back into dry clothes. When we went to wake Tim to find out if the food were cooked, he pushed us away, rolled over, and went back to sleep again. His rheumatism medicine was all gone, and the pint bottle in which he carried it lay open by his side.

"Let him sleep it off," Dad advised. "Come on, let's eat." We lifted off the seaweed with sticks, and I've never smelled or tasted anything more delicious than those clams, lobsters, and corn. Tim had planned for nine adults, instead of one adult and eight children, but we ate until we were stuffed and there was nothing left except shells and cobs.

It was beginning to get dark, and fog had started to roll in, by the time we had buried the last of the cobs, thrown the shells into the water, and otherwise cleaned up the beach. But when Dad went over to wake up the captain, Tim wouldn't budge. He was snoring loudly now, and even when Dad shook him he didn't open his eyes.

"Come on, man, stop playing possum and wake up," Dad insisted, "I've got to get my kids home. Come on, now. No more foolishness."

"Is he dead, Daddy?" a young brother asked casually.

"Dead drunk," an older sister explained knowingly.
"Dead men don't snore. He's stewed to the eyebrows, isn't
he Dad?"

"If you don't get on your feet right now and stop this
nonsense," said Dad, "I'm going to leave you right here
and sail your boat back without you."

"Could you do that, Daddy?" I asked eagerly. "Do you
know enough to sail her home without him?"

"Sure you could, couldn't you Daddy?" boasted a
younger brother.

"Well," Dad said carefully, "I *think* I could. I've never
done it—or at least not for years. But I know *how* it's
done."

"Let's leave him," said the young brother. "He's just an
old grouch, anyway. Can I be the first mate, Daddy?"

"Wake up," Dad insisted, shaking the captain again. But
the idea of sailing the *Minnie R.* triumphantly back to
Nantucket must have been working in the back of Dad's
mind. Because immediately he started falling into nautical
terms.

"Yes sir," said Dad, giving the captain still another
shake, "if you don't get up and take command right now,
I'll relieve you, sir. I'll maroon you here on the beach, and
seize the vessel. Get up, I say. Avast, there."

But it soon became obvious that neither threats nor
pleadings would cause Tim to stir. And it was now quite
dark and cool.

"Let's go, Daddy," we urged. "Let's maroon him, like
you said."

"No, we can't leave him," said Dad. "He's too old. He

might catch pneumonia. See if you can help me get him on my back."

We helped pick the captain up, and Dad finally got him across his shoulders, in a fireman's lift, and waded out to the boat. Dad dumped Tim on the deck, and then as gently as we could we dragged him into the cabin.

Dad took his place at the helm, cast a sharp weather eye at the wind pennant, and barked out his orders.

"Hoist the mains'il," he commanded. "Up with the throat. Up with the peak."

Here again was the sort of situation which Dad enjoyed playing to the hilt, and he made the most of it.

"Look alive, you lubbers," he shouted. "Haul away on those halyards. Pull up the anchor. Look out for the boom. Here we go."

He was correct in saying that we were going, but where we went was right up on the beach. The *Minnie R.* went hard aground, and we all had to get out and push her off.

But finally we were underway at last, in the moonlight. Luckily the wind was blowing gently and right toward Nantucket, so very little seamanship was required. It had turned cold, but it wasn't so bad when we all huddled together around Dad in the stern. He let me take the wheel while he went into the cabin, covered Tim with a blanket, and brought out some other blankets for us. We wrapped up in them, and pretty soon we were warm. The stars were out bright and Dad pretended that he was charting his course by the Big Dipper, but we all knew that really he was sailing for Brant Point light, which could be seen plainly across the harbor in the distance.

"Daddy is the best captain on all Nantucket, eh Daddy?"

a young brother announced. "We're going like sixty, eh
Captain Daddy?"

"I'll tell the cockeyed world," Dad agreed quietly. "And
I've got the best crew on all Nantucket, too, eh live bait?"

We said we'd tell the cockeyed world.

"I'll swear," Dad joked, "I've got such a bully crew that
if there were any of that rheumatism medicine left, I'd
serve an extra tot of rum to all hands and the cook—no, to
all hands *except* the cook."

The *Minnie R.*, however sedate, nevertheless managed
to kick up a slight wake which glowed phosphorescently.
We sang "Moonlight Bay" and "Over There." And then
Dad taught us what he said was a pirate chanty which
went, "Fifteen men on a dead man's chest, yo-ho-ho and
a bottle of rheumatism medicine."

Ah, those were the days all right!

I ought to say, in Cap'n Tim's behalf, that he didn't
make a practice of getting loaded on the job. He was
downright sheepish when he came over to our cottage next
day and apologized to Dad. We had left the *Minnie R.*
berthed at the wharf, with Tim still asleep below. Luckily,
he didn't realize that he hadn't been at the wheel, when
Dad rammed the dock so hard he broke the forestay.

"I don't recollect the trip home very well," Tim conceded. "I shouldn't have drunk so much, with all your
kids aboard, and I'm sorry. What did I do—sail right up
to the dock before the wind? Any fool, no matter how
drunk, had ought to know better than that."

"Something like that," Dad agreed.

"I'd like to give you back your money, if you'd take it."

"Forget it," said Dad. "You'll need the money to get a new stay."

Tim went to his reward about five years ago, and I saw him the summer before he died. He was sitting on a bench in the shade of one of the wineglass elm trees on Main Street, in front of Roger's Store where everyone comes to get the newspapers from the mainland.

He was incredibly old, then, and his nose if anything was even redder than I remembered it. I sat down by him, and he smelled as if he had been doctoring his rheumatism.

It is the almost unanimous belief of visitors that the surest way to flatter an old resident of any resort is to ask him for a weather forecast. The visitors seldom place the least bit of credence in such forecasts, but they dutifully request them, just the same.

Not being able to think of anything else to say, I too automatically asked the stock question:

"What kind of weather will we have tomorrow, Cap'n?"

I don't know whether or not Tim recognized me, but at any rate he looked me over none too affectionately, spat some tobacco juice which scored a near miss on my dark blue sneakers, and replied in a loud and sarcastic voice designed to discourage similar asinine questions from me and other summer visitors in the vicinity:

"Don't ask me, Johnny. My radio's broke, and I ain't heard the latest report."

12. MR. MACY MAKES GOOD

The *Rena*, which my father acquired not long after our squantum at Coatue, also was a catboat, but not so large as the *Minnie R*. We moored her off the beach in front of our cottage and, although she was old and battered, Dad kept her polished and glistening with paint. We were all mighty proud of the *Rena,* and there wasn't a more ship-shape boat in the harbor.

I wasn't old enough to sail her, but I used to wade out to her and tinker around—pump her out, polish her brass, re-coil her ropes, and sit at the tiller and make believe I was her skipper.

After we had had the *Rena* for about three weeks, I was sponging out the last drop of water in her bilge one evening when I discovered a plug in her side, just above the waterline. I pulled the plug out experimentally, and forgot to put it back.

It rained hard that night, and as the weight of the rain water caused the *Rena* to settle, the hole where the plug had been let the sea water come in. By morning, the *Rena's* deck was awash.

We helped Dad bring her toward shore to pump her out and he was upset to say the least. When we had about half the water out, we got some rollers under her and dragged her up on the beach. Then, of course, the water flowed out of the hole in her side—and for the first time I realized I was the one who had sunk the *Rena*.

"Well, that's why she sank," said Dad. "I wonder what lame-brained idiot pulled out that plug. It couldn't have worked loose by itself, because I examined it carefully a couple of days ago." The more he thought it over, the angrier he got. "I'd like to get my hands on the vicious vandal," he told us. "I don't know why people do things like that—deliberately damage other people's property. Probably some juvenile delinquent from downtown."

My conscience told me to speak up, but my common sense advised me to stand mute, so I compromised.

"It couldn't have come out by itself, there's no doubt about that," I agreed. "Someone must have pulled it out."

"I'd like to break every bone in his body," muttered Dad. "Look at those charts of mine in the cabin. Ruined!"

So I know just how Love Paddock must have felt in the early days of Nantucket. Love married George Swain, raised a family, and was a respected member of the community. When she was an old woman of eighty-one and very sick, Mrs. Swain asked that the neighbors be summoned to hear something of great importance that she wanted to get off her chest before Crossing the Bar.

Old Aunt Love had been put to bed in the combination bornin' and dyin' room of her gray, shingled house. And since a woman of eighty-one is not likely to be using a bornin'-dyin' room for the purpose of having a blessed event, there was no doubt in her mind that her number was up.

When the neighbors were standing around her bed, Aunt Love propped herself up on her pillow and said:

"All of thee have heard about the time, seventy years ago, when someone drained Lily Pond and did all that terrible damage."

The neighbors nodded solemnly.

"I," Aunt Love disclosed dramatically, "am that somebody."

The neighbors gasped in disbelief, because the mystery of the pond-draining had intrigued the island for three generations. But Aunt Love confessed to the whole story before she died, and old Obed Macy, the historian, subsequently recorded the story in a manuscript that never was published.

Love Paddock was eleven years old at the time, and lived in a house on a hill which formed the north side of Lily Pond. The pond itself is only about a hundred yards from the ocean.

She was returning home from a neighbor's house one afternoon, when she noticed that the water in the pond was unusually high. Taking a clam shell, Love made a little gutter all the way from the pond to the ocean, to see the water flow. It flowed only at a trickle, and it never occurred to her that since the tide was out and the pond was high, the big pond might drain.

So she went home to supper, giving no further thought to the little ditch which, child-like, she had dug.

But the next morning she was awakened by loud roars from her father, who had looked out the window and seen the empty pond. Historian Macy wrote that the conversation went like this:

"O, what a wicked piece of work is here!" said her father.

"What is it?" Love's mother asked.

"Some evil-minded person has let Lily Pond out."

"But who would do a terrible thing like that?"

"It has carried away the sand and made a great gully," Mr. Paddock continued. "The mill is gone and the fences torn up. Several small vessels which lay up in the creek to winter have been damaged and some boats stove to pieces. . . ."

Young Love decided, after overhearing the conversation, that nothing she could say would repair the damage. So, quite wisely, she said nothing.

Besides, as she pointed out to the neighbors around her death bed, although the matter had bothered her conscience for seventy years, she never had really lied about it.

"You see," said Aunt Love innocently, "nobody ever asked me if I was the one who did the damage."

A contemporary of Aunt Love's was a spinster known as Cousin Phebe, who was both deeply religious, and deeply superstitious. Like many non-Quaker islanders of her day, she believed that Nantucket's twisted wild-hawthorn trees which dance eerily on windy, moonlit nights are the spirits of unhappy old maids who must live through eternity without a mate. She also concurred in the belief that a black cat, placed under a washtub, would cause strong enough headwinds to prevent ships sailing from the harbor.

Cousin Phebe was odd, not especially attractive, and had a terrible dread of ending up an old maid. Although she set her cap for a number of bachelors—and delayed their sailings by duly smothering black cats—no man had ever paid her more than passing attention.

Incidentally, since women on Nantucket outnumbered men by about four to one at the time, there was a continuing demand for black cats. The animals were rare and their life expectancy was brief. Maltese cats also were considered by some women to be just about as effective as black cats.

The superstition about the Maltese variety gained credence when the Schooner *William E. Callis* sailed from Nantucket for New York with a cargo which included fifty of the Maltese. The vessel ran into such rugged weather that she had to put into Martha's Vineyard for repairs. Then, when she set out for New York again, she encountered more stormy weather and head winds. Finally, in desperation, the sailors threw the cats overboard. Almost immediately, the weather cleared, the winds shifted, and there was smooth sailing all the way to New York. Things weren't so smooth, though, when the man who owned the cats found out what had happened to them. He sued the *Callis* for $50 for each animal.

Getting back to Cousin Phebe, she was walking on the

moors one fateful evening, and stopped to admire a beautiful sunset. But her admiration turned to despair, and a
chill went up her spine, when she saw that one lone wild-
hawthorn tree stood in gnarled relief between her and
the fiery ball of the sun, on the horizon. As the sun disappeared, the color of the tree changed from crimson to a
depressing gray.

Cousin Phebe said later she was sure that God had sent
her a revelation—that she would die an unhappy old maid
unless she took prompt action.

She ran hysterically to the tree, fell down on her knees,
and promised the Lord that she would propose to the very
next bachelor she saw.

She was horrified, on getting to her feet, to observe a
dilapidated wagon coming along a rutted road on the
moors. The wagon was pulled by a goat, with an assist
from a patched sail. Everyone on Nantucket was familiar
with the wagon, and knew that it belonged to James Newbegin, bachelor and village half-wit.

Cousin Phebe rationalized for a moment that, whereas
she had seen the wagon, she hadn't actually seen James
—and therefore wasn't obligated to propose to him. But
just as she was about to pick up her skirts and run, James'
head appeared under the sail, he hallooed at her, and she
was honest enough to concede to herself that church was
out. James altered course, and steered the goat cart up to
Phebe.

"Evenin', Cousin Phebe," he grinned vacantly. "Can I
give thee a ride?"

"I expect so," she sighed with resignation. "James, will
you marry me?"

And so they were married, and lived "out Madaket way" in a filthy one-room shack James owned. They had three daughters—shy creatures who would run and hide if visitors approached the house. James and Phebe died within a few months of each other, when the oldest girl, named for her mother, was about fifteen. The townspeople repeatedly brought the Newbegin girls to Nantucket and put them in decent homes. But the girls would always run away and go back to their shack, which was overrun by pet hens, each with a Biblical name, and anonymous cats. The girls grew their own vegetables and sold the eggs produced by Salome, Rebecca, Mary Magdalen et al. Finally, the townspeople gave up and decided to let the girls shift for themselves.

By the time Phebe was twenty and the other girls were in their late teens, they had conquered their shyness enough so that they sometimes came to town voluntarily. Phebe was strikingly handsome, but she was so queer and her family had been the object of scorn and pity for so long that no Nantucket man had anything to do with her. The other two girls, although far from ugly, were a trifle heavy-set and seemed plain in comparison with their beautiful sister.

In those days, thousands of sheep grazed the moors, and a big festival was held annually at shearing time. The year that Phebe was twenty, the girls happened to be in town on an egg-selling expedition, at the time of the festival, and they edged up to the crowd to see what was going on. They were entranced, and remained on the outskirts of the throng until well after dark.

A handsome off-island sailor named Dudley, slightly in

his cups and behaving in an extremely un-Quaker manner, wandered through the crowd telling every girl how beautiful she was and kissing those who would let him. Somehow or other, he managed to kiss all three of the Newbegin girls. Phebe's beauty made such an impression on him that he impulsively took off a silver scarf pin he was wearing, and pinned it to her bosom.

That night, when they went back to their shack, each of the girls put a black cat under a tub. In the morning, there were three dead cats—but head winds didn't develop, and Dudley sailed away.

Each sister thought he was in love with her—and all three waited for him, and waited, and waited—and became more and more odd with the passing years.

They developed a number of weird rituals that they would go through every day, regardless of the weather. There was a big rock in front of their shack, and they would march around it, thirty or forty times, at sunrise and sunset. When they went from the house to their pump, they made three turns around every post. On the infrequent occasions when they came to town, they would tack back and forth across the street if the wind were against them, and go forward in a straight line at a half-run if the wind were at their backs. They didn't bother to wash or to comb their hair, and they seemed to hate each other.

"They think a certain sailor boy is coming back to marry them," the youngest and most talkative of the three sometimes would whisper to a Nantucket woman. "Don't tell them this, because it would break their hearts. But he's really coming back to marry me."

Dudley didn't return to Nantucket for forty years. He

was a captain then, and planning to retire, but Phebe had made such an impression on him that he decided to look her up. After getting directions from an amused townsman, Dudley started to walk out the Madaket road.

It happened that the youngest sister had been in town to sell some eggs, and was on the way home. Coming up behind her and of course not realizing who she was, Dudley was amazed to see the unkempt hag tack from one side of the road to the other, and pause occasionally to make three solemn turns around a post. He caught up with her just as she arrived at her shack. The door was open, and he could see two other hags inside, staring vacantly into space. Hens were perched on a bureau, and on the beds, and one hen appeared to be laying in a bureau drawer.

He was about to ask the woman he had followed for directions to the Newbegin residence, when she ran to the rock in front of the shack and started loping around it. The other two quickly joined her in the mad circling.

And with a shiver of horror, Dudley saw that the oldest of the hags wore "on her withered bosom" a silver scarf pin that had been his forty years ago.

He returned quickly to his ship and never came back to Nantucket again.

Every previous story I've told about Nantucket has been pretty thoroughly documented. But I'll have to admit that the story of the Newbegin girls—although it appeared sixty years ago in *The Atlantic Monthly* and subsequently was given tacit endorsement by being published in book form by no less an organization than the Nantucket Goldenrod Literary and Debating Society—seems too pat to be true.

There is no doubt, though, that the Newbegin girls actually existed and were even odder than huckleberry chowder, because I've found any number of references to them in the old books.

Today, a little off the road to Madaket, three twisted old wild hawthorn trees are growing in a line by a rock. I wish they were in a circle instead of a line! Nantucketers will tell you with a straight face—but that doesn't mean anything, because when a Nantucketer decides to tell summer visitors a tall story his face is almost *always* straight—that the three trees which dance tortuously on windy, moonlit nights are growing at the exact spot where the Newbegin girls' shack used to be.

Since this chapter already is something of a potpourri, I may as well complete the mixture by adding a few more miscellaneous Nantucketers.

For instance, there was Benny Cleveland, whose house still stands in Eagle Lane. Benny was a jack-of-all-trades, and specialized in doing odd jobs for women whose husbands were away at sea. He was a rather vague citizen, and so innocent and harmless that no scandal could ever attach itself to him. As a result, when women were ill or expecting babies, and their husbands were away, they sometimes hired Benny to sleep in their houses.

Looking for more business along this line, Benny ran a newspaper advertisement which has become something of a classic:

"Women slept with, twenty-five cents a night," said the ad. "Nervous women, fifteen cents extra."

Nantucket's best-known newspaper editor was Samuel Haynes Jenks of *The Inquirer*. He had a sense of humor and a thick hide, and liked to write punning poetry about local weddings. For example, when Lydia B. Long married Barnabas Bourne, Jenks wrote:

> Said the bridegroom in haste to his bride elect,
> Don't Lydia B. Long, for the torch of love burns;
> But the damsel more wary and circumspect asked
> If this was the Bourne whence no trav'ler returns.

In September 1826, some people who didn't like Jenks' politics started a newspaper named *The Journal*. William H. Bigelow was hired as editor of *The Journal* and, for some reason that I can't figure out, persisted in spelling *The Inquirer* as *The Enquirer*.

The capital "E" irritated Jenks, but he was an advocate of the soft answer. He wrote mildly that Mr. Bigelow must "find himself ill at 'E's, putting out other people's 'I's."

In the 1880's, the Governor of Massachusetts, Oliver Ames, came to Nantucket to marry Anna Ray Swain. As he was walking up Main Street, the governor was stopped by a Nantucketer.

"I presume likely you came to Nantucket for the big wedding," the Nantucketer remarked conversationally.

"Whose wedding?" asked the governor, confidently expecting to hear his praises sung.

"Why Anna Ray's, of course. She's a Swain, you know."

"Do tell," said the governor. Then he added hopefully, "But whom is she marrying?"

"Someone from off," the Nantucketer shrugged. "I forget his name."

Daniel Webster, who was a pretty shrewd bargainer himself, nevertheless "got took" on Nantucket. Webster was once asked by a Nantucket Quaker how much he'd charge to argue a case in court on the island. Webster said his fee would be $500, and although the amount seemed staggering the islander finally hired him with the stipulation that Dan'l would handle not only that case but whatever other business the Quaker might have at that term of court.

The Quaker then went around Nantucket offering to sell the services of the great lawyer for fees as low as $50. When Webster arrived on the island, he found that his client was involved in almost every case on the docket, and Dan'l had to work day and night for a couple of weeks preparing and presenting his court arguments. The Quaker not only managed to have his own case argued for nothing, but actually made a profit on the deal.

Rowland Hussey Macy, who was born on Nantucket August 20, 1822, was descended directly by four different lines from Thomas Macy, the first settler. Rowland's father, John, was the captain of a merchant ship for a time, and then operated a book and magazine store at 2 Fair Street.

Rowland went to sea on the whaler *Emily Morgan* when he was fifteen and the ship ran into greasy luck in the Pacific. When she returned home four years later, she had three thousand barrels of oil, one thousand pounds of whale bone, and two hundred and fifty pounds of ambergris. Young Macy's "lay" for the four years was $500.

Later, he went to Boston, married the daughter of a dry-goods merchant, opened his own store, and failed. After a year or two, he opened another store in Boston, and failed again.

Then he and his brother Charles headed for California in the Gold Rush. They sailed for Panama in March, 1849 on the brig *Dr. Hitchcock*, made the perilous trip across the Isthmus on muleback, and took the Steamer *Sylph* to San Francisco. Instead of mining gold, Rowland opened a general store in Maryville, Calif. He failed again.

He came back home from the "gold diggin's" in 1851, settled in Haverhill, Mass., and opened the Haverhill Cheap Store. That failed, too—but not until Macy had experimented with some policies that revolutionized retailing around the world.

Those policies were buying for cash, selling for cash with a small markup, keeping goods moving, using extensive newspaper advertising, and having one price for everybody.

Macy probably didn't originate any of those policies, but he was the first to employ a combination of all of them. The policies seem routine enough today, but before the Civil War most retail businesses worked on credit, and because of a series of depressions many accounts weren't paid. Consequently, prices were kept high to compensate for losses caused by bad debts. Also, the general practice of storekeepers was to quote purposely inflated prices on all articles, so that shoppers could have the satisfaction of "beating down" the price to a "bargain" level.

As Macy explained in a newspaper ad for the Haverhill Cheap Store, "By adopting one price and never deviating, a child can trade with us as cheap as the shrewdest buyer in the country."

In other ads, the Quaker merchant from Nantucket told residents of Haverhill that it was wise to save money and that he would not let any merchant in town—or in Boston either—undersell him. Even in 1852, R. H. Macy believed that "It's Smart to Be Thrifty."

Haverhill was too small a town to provide the turnover needed for Rowland's small-markups, and the Cheap Store folded in 1855. Rowland went to Superior City, Wisconsin, as a real-estate broker and land speculator. He failed again.

Then he came back East and, in 1858, opened in New York City a little hole-in-the-wall called Macy's, on the east side of Sixth Avenue (Avenue of the Americas), one door below Fourteenth Street. He had a frontage of less than twenty feet, and his store was only sixty feet deep. His stock was fancy drygoods—handkerchiefs, ribbons, laces, feathers, and ladies' gloves and stockings. His first day's sales amounted to $11.06.

But the bearded Nantucketer—who someplace along the line had lost his Quaker religion but not his Quaker integrity—found New York to be ready made for him. Macy smoked cigars, occasionally swore like a New Bedford dockhand, and indulged in flamboyant advertising. But just the same, he remembered and practiced the maxims about thrift, honesty, and industry.

When he advertised the retail policies that he had tried out experimentally in Haverhill, his New York competitors chuckled, and predicted that he wouldn't be around very long. They told each other cynically, but perhaps with some truth, that because of all his previous failures, he *had* to buy and sell for cash: That no wholesaler or manufacturer would allow him credit, and that he had to collect immediately for his sales so as to pay the rent.

Nevertheless, Macy's prospered almost from the start. A year after the store opened, Rowland—who never was much of a sailor and got no higher than forecastle hand on the *Emily Morgan*—was known throughout the retail district as "Captain" Macy. Apparently he liked to play the part of a seadog, because his advertising in 1859 was salted with ship-talk.

"Trade is good at Macy's and they are happy as clams at high water at Macy's," one ad says. "Go, all hands, go in together, and be happy at Macy's."

In 1860, he hired a one-eyed Nantucket school teacher named Margaret Getchell to keep his accounts and to help him watch the cash drawer. Between them, they expanded Macy's to a department store and worked out the odd-penny price system, under which $4 items were priced at $3.98, $10.50 items at $10.47, and so forth. The psychology of making a price look lower was, of course, the basic reason for this.

But Margaret had another reason, too. Prices at odd pennies usually meant that salesclerks had to make change, and thus Margaret could be sure, when the salesclerks came to the cash drawer, that they turned in the money they had received.

When Margaret married a man named Abiel La Forge, Macy gave him a job so that the bride wouldn't quit. The newlyweds took a flat above the store, and Macy came to rely so strongly on both of them that he made Abiel a partner.

Margaret herself was probably the first American woman to hold down an executive job in big business. Macy, having grown up on Nantucket where women were accustomed to handling financial affairs, had as much respect for her ability as he would have had for any man's. And he was also smart enough to realize that, since women were beginning to do most of the shopping in this country, a woman's touch was needed in the store.

Fifteen years after he had started his business in New York, Macy had acquired eleven adjoining stores and was the city's second largest retailer. And although he stopped swearing when he finally got religion again at a Moody and Sankey revival, his temper was notorious. Once when a customer complained that the handle of her new umbrella broke off as soon as she walked out of the store, Macy shouted that her claim was ridiculous and indignantly led her to the umbrella counter to demonstrate that his goods were as strong as iron. Confidently, he tested a handle there, and when it broke too, and the lady tittered, he flew into a rage and twisted to pieces every umbrella on the counter.

He also refused to have shades on any of the gas lamps in the store, because he said that shades curtailed the light. Nantucket-fashion, he asserted that he intended to have all the illumination he paid for. Once when he found that shades were being installed despite his orders, he grabbed a hammer from a workman and stalked angrily around the store breaking them.

Macy died in 1877, while in Paris on a buying trip. The present owners of the store, the Strauses, became partners in 1888 and full owners in 1896. They moved Macy's to Herald Square in 1902.

But the Strauses themselves are among the first to admit that a former Nantucket whaleman and a former Nantucket school teacher built the foundation of the "biggest store in the world," on the Quaker principles of integrity and hard work.

13. MARIA AND THE COMET

Maria Mitchell was the Nantucket Quaker girl who discovered a comet from the roof of her father's bank, and thus made headlines around the world. Today, her birthplace on Vestal Street is maintained as a memorial. In the side yard is a small observatory, presided over by Miss Margaret Harwood, a remarkable and ageless woman who taught navigation to naval officers in both World Wars. Miss Harwood's special astronomy project for forty years or so has been to keep an eye on Eros, a variable asteroid.

It goes without saying that since an observatory was right there on the island, astronomy became a required course on the curricula of my father's program of summer education.

The first time I ever saw the beautiful ring around

Saturn was as a young boy, through Miss Harwood's tele-scope. I suppose she has shown the stars to twenty thou-sand children since then. Like Maria, Miss Harwood is a natural-born teacher and possesses a warm personality and a sharp wit—and her tongue is not dull.

I remember that I was in an uncooperative mood when my father hoisted me up to the telescope's eyepiece to see Saturn, because whereas I had wanted Dad to take us to the movies, he had decided the night was ideal for as-tronomy.

I kept up a running commentary about how movies were better than stars. Then, when I looked through the eyepiece, I could see only a blank white circle.

"This old telescope must be broken," I pouted. "I don't see why we had to come here in the first place, when there was a movie with . . ."

"Young man," said Miss Harwood firmly but not un-kindly, "if you would open your eyes a little wider and close your lips a little tighter, you might see Saturn."

I followed her suggestion, and I saw Saturn. If Miss Harwood had used a couple of "thees" and "thous" for her "yous," it might have been Maria Mitchell talking.

Maria came into the world in 1818, in the small bornin' room of the Vestal Street house. Her mother had been a librarian before she married, and her father was a justice of the peace who did astronomical observations for the Coast Survey, rated chronometers for mariners, and served as cashier of the Pacific Bank.

By the time Maria was twelve, she was helping her fa-ther to make his astronomical observations, and already had amazed at least one sea captain by correcting his chronometer, in the absence of Mr. Mitchell. At sixteen, she knew as much about mathematics and the stars as her father. At seventeen, she opened a private school for children, and at eighteen she was made librarian of the Atheneum, at a salary of sixty dollars a year—a little over a dollar a week.

At the library, Maria taught many a future captain the rudiments of navigation and how to use Bowditch's tables. To make certain that Nantucket children didn't waste their time reading "trash," she hid all the books she considered objectionable, returning them to the shelves only for the annual inspections by the Atheneum trustees.

A painting of Miss Mitchell, as a formidable old spinster, hangs today on the walls of the library. Her white hair is arranged in rather prim curls over a high and furrowed brow, her eyes are dark and searching, and her mouth and nose both are a little too big to be handsome. One gets the impression, even from the picture, that Miss Mitchell doesn't intend to put up with any nonsense, and that if there is any giggling or whispering she'll step right out of the frame and shush the offenders.

When I used to go to the Atheneum to read Zane Grey westerns and books about boys' boarding schools by Ralph Henry Barbour, I sometimes wished they'd turn Miss Mitchell's grim visage toward the wall. Her picture made me feel as if I should be boning up on history and spelling, in preparation for next autumn's classes, instead of frittering away my time with steely-eyed Dale Horn, who was lightnin' fast on the draw, and Harry Gilbert, a three-letter man who gave the school bully his lumps.

As a young woman, Maria was raven haired, raw boned,

and tart as a crabapple. According to her own testimony, she was downright ugly, but that must have been Quaker modesty. Her early pictures show that while certainly no beauty, and admittedly a trifle on the grim side, she carried herself well and had a self-assured dignity which made her stand out as a Somebody.

Although the prim curls in the Atheneum painting belie it, Miss Mitchell apparently never gave much thought to her appearance. When a friend stopped her on the street once to remark, "Maria, thee has a hole in thy stocking," she replied icily, "Only one?" She wore shoes a couple of sizes too large for her, because they felt more comfortable that way. And once at a tea party, when a prissy acquaintance came over to her and with some distaste picked a thread from her wrinkled dress, Maria snapped angrily, "Please put that thread back where it came from."

The same year that Maria became librarian at the Atheneum she moved with her parents and eight brothers and sisters to living quarters on the second story of the Pacific Bank. The red-brick bank, now mellowed to the color of dying embers, is operating today under that same name—a name which it took because most of Nantucket's wealth came from Pacific whales. The bank stands in cobblestoned Main Street, at the point where the street leaves the old residential district, widens, and becomes for two blocks an elm-shaded and still cobblestoned retail business district.

On the roof of the bank, Mr. Mitchell set up his four-inch brass telescope, and nightly Maria climbed through the "scuttle" of the roof to help her father do his observation work for the Coast Survey. Then, she'd "sweep" the heavens for her own record books. In winter, she wore what she called her "regimentals"—hood, greatcoat and boots—but even so her nose was occasionally frostbitten.

Maria's mathematical mind demanded a precise answer for everything, and no subject was deemed immune from probing questions. As a girl, she accepted the rigors of Quaker discipline. But as a young and strong-willed woman, she decided that some of the Quaker taboos were senseless.

She and her sisters used to entertain themselves on stormy nights by seeing who could memorize certain classical poems the quickest. Understandably, Maria came to the eventual conclusion that this pastime was neither the gayest nor the most exciting recreation in the world.

So one day, during her parents' absence, Maria had a piano moved into their living quarters above the bank. And when her parents returned home later that afternoon, they found the children gathered around the piano, with one sister picking out a tune and all the other children singing.

Mrs. Mitchell didn't approve at all, but Mr. Mitchell had long been of the opinion that there was no harm in music and that Quakerism was too strict. Instead of protesting, he joined in the songs. You could hear the music and singing up and down Main Street, and the neighbors were so shocked that Mr. Mitchell was quickly placed "under dealings."

Luckily, Mr. Mitchell was an influential man in the community, and as cashier of the bank he also was custodian of the Meeting House property. When the members of the Select Committee came to reprimand him, he told them in effect that if they wouldn't let his children keep a piano, he'd stop being a Friend.

The decline of Quakerism already had begun, and the Select Committeemen apparently decided that they couldn't afford to lose the Mitchells. So the piano stayed, and Mr. Mitchell wasn't even required to make a humiliating confession of error at the Meeting.

Around the same time, Maria took up the extremely un-Friendly pastime of playing cards. "Last night," she wrote in her diary, "I took my first lesson in whist playing. I learned in one evening to tell the King, Queen, and Jack apart, and to understand what my partner meant when she winked at me."

A person with Maria's questioning mind would not long feel at home within the rigid confines of the Friends' religion. And when she was twenty-five years old, the librarian and girl astronomer admitted honestly to a Select Committee that her mind was "not settled" on religious subjects. At the next meeting, she was disowned without further ado. Thereafter, she attended—but apparently never joined—the Unitarian Church. At heart, though, Maria always remained a Quaker—even though she disapproved of their nonsensical bans against innocent pleasures.

She discovered her comet when she was twenty-nine, through her father's telescope on top of the bank. She was "sweeping" the sky at the time, and happened to find something that at first looked like a nebula—at a place where no nebula had a right to be. Feeling sure it must be a comet, she raced down through the scuttle in the roof and, still in her "regimentals," almost literally pulled her father away from a "gay" Quaker party which was in progress below.

Mr. Mitchell, once he got the idea of why Maria wanted him, didn't have to be pulled. Back through the scuttle crawled Maria, with her father hot at her heels. He looked through the telescope and confirmed her discovery.

All of that happened on October 1, 1847, and the date is significant. Because on October 3, the comet was "discovered" in Rome, and on October 7 it was "discovered" in England, and on October 11 it was "discovered" in Hamburg, and around the same time Harvard University Observatory started keeping an eye on it.

It so happened that, as every astronomer of the time knew, King Frederic VI of Denmark had offered in 1831 an expensive gold medal to the first person who discovered a comet which could not be seen with the naked eye. The King had further specified—quite wisely, in order to prevent Johnny-come-latelies from post-dating their discoveries—that a report of a comet had to be mailed by *first post* after discovery.

Nantucket is a long way from the mainland and an even longer way from Denmark, so a number of weeks passed before the Mitchells were sure even that Maria had been the first American to see the comet—let alone the first person in the whole world. As a matter of fact, the King of Denmark didn't issue the gold medal until October 6, 1848—a little more than a year after Maria's discovery— when he finally became convinced that she had first claim.

Well, you know how the newspapers are: "Lady Star-Gazer Discovers Comet," "Nantucket Lady Honored by

King" and all that sort of thing. Overnight, tart-tongued but retiring Maria Mitchell—a Plain Jane if ever there was one—became an international celebrity.

The "Women of America" subscribed money to buy her a new five-inch telescope which she set up in an observatory built behind the Coffin School. In spite of the die-hard objections of Asa Gray, Harvard botanist who thought Woman's Place Was in the Home, she was elected the first Honorary Fellow of the American Academy of Arts and Sciences. Even after Maria's election, old Dr. Gray, who was secretary of the academy, stubbornly crossed out the word "Fellow" after her name on the membership roll, and substituted "Honorary Member." But that didn't change the fact that she had been elected, indeed, a "Fellow."

Under the sponsorship of Louis Agassiz, she was also elected to the Association for the Advancement of Science. She toured Europe, visiting most of the observatories there, and when she returned to the United States she was given a job at five hundred dollars a year to make astronomical calculations for the *Nautical Almanac*.

Some years later, when Matthew Vassar was founding his college for females, *Godey's Lady Book* asserted editorially that it would be a great pity if Mr. Vassar were unable "to find a lady in the United States qualified to instruct her own sex in the higher branches of science and learning."

Godey's, besides being the ladies' fashion bible, also was a champion of women's rights. Among other things, *Godey's* deplored a stock joke which kept cropping up in newspapers and men's publications, wherein a suffragette matron was supposed to ask her audience, "What is home without a mother?" and a voice from the back of the auditorium to shout in impolite reply, "Your children."

It is not clear whether *Godey's* needling had any effect on Mr. Vassar, but at any rate Maria was offered in 1864 the position of Professor of Astronomy and Director of the Vassar Observatory. The salary was to be $1,500 a year.

Maria promptly wrote to Rufus Babcock, a college trustee, "I had not thought of so large a sum as $1,500. I do not believe I am worth it."

Nevertheless, although she had some qualms about whether she would be a good teacher, she went to Poughkeepsie and accepted the job and the salary. As it turned out, she needn't have worried about her ability, because she became one of the best—and most unorthodox—teachers in the history of the college. There must have been times, though, when the Vassar officials wished they had never hired her.

Hating needless regimentation, she paid no attention whatsoever to the college rules. Although the girls had to be in bed at an early hour, Professor Mitchell thought nothing of racing through the dormitory in her regimentals at three or four o'clock in the morning, and awakening and rooting out all the twittering young females to see a spectacular display of shooting stars.

As for giving grades to her pupils, Maria had her own unique standards. Often the best grade went to some girl who had had the courage to show up completely unprepared and empty-headed for Professor Mitchell's classes. To face Maria unprepared must have required a great deal of courage indeed, because as she grew older she became more outspoken, more independent, more tart tongued, and more imposing than ever before—which was considerable.

Until the new girls got to know her and discovered the warmth of her personality, they were frankly scared to death of her. And so were most of the other teachers and so, I suspect, was President John Howard Raymond.

Once when a young teacher told Professor Mitchell that her shawl was brushing the ground, Maria—who didn't like to be fussed over—snapped that "If my shawl drags, I want it to."

And when a student, seeking to curry favor, said she knew quite well one of Professor Mitchell's cousins on Nantucket, Maria replied coldly, "I have five thousand cousins there." This statement, as a matter of fact, was probably completely accurate, since almost everyone on Nantucket was related.

Maria begrudged the time she had to spend preparing routine annual reports on her department, for President Raymond. She felt that the compilation interferred both with her teaching and with her observatory work.

One year, as she placed her report on the president's desk, she inquired:

"And into the oblivion of whose hands do I consign this paper?"

"Mine," blushed President Raymond.

Being an intelligent man, the president well realized what a splendid teacher Maria was. Being also well aware of her tart tongue, he did his best not to notice her infraction of rules or her occasional disdain of conventions. However, Maria engaged more or less continually in one practice which drew criticism both from townspeople and from visiting parents. And finally President Raymond had to take action.

With "deference and reluctance," he finally went to Professor Mitchell to bell the cat. If she found it necessary to mend her, ahem, stockings and other, ahem, garments on Sunday, he asked, would she mind not sitting so close to the observatory windows?

Maria replied that so far as her conscience was concerned, it was perfectly all right to mend, ahem, anything she felt like mending on Sunday, and that since her conscience allowed her to mend, she proposed to continue to mend where there was the best light.

The next Sunday she moved her chair up even closer to the window.

The Lady Astronomer Who Discovered a Comet died in 1889. If you want to read more about her, I recommend a fascinating biography called *Sweeper in the Sky*, by Helen Wright. Miss Wright says that Maria's last words—delivered, I'm sure, with a snort—were:

"Well, if this is dying, there's nothing very unpleasant about it."

14. DECLINE AND FALL OF A
WHALING TOWN

Nantucket's most prosperous era began on a snowy January day in 1815, when a packet arrived in the harbor with news that the War of 1812 had ended.

Like the Revolution, the War of 1812 had brought hunger and hardships to Nantucket, where more than half of the vessels had been seized and hundreds of seamen impressed. Word of the Peace Treaty of Ghent was so wonderfully welcome that it touched off a "general jollification" such as the Quaker town had never seen before.

Jonathan Parker lashed a jury-rigged mast onto his peat sled, hoisted Old Glory, and drove all over the island spreading the happy news. Bonfires blazed up in Main Street. Men and boys raced through the streets shooting muskets and pistols. Quaker ladies bustled from bonfire to bonfire with steaming pots of tea and crisp "wonders"— as the islanders called doughnuts.

If all of that still doesn't seem to add up to much of a jollification, at any rate the Quakers thought they were really letting down their hair.

A few weeks later, the Unitarians proudly mounted in the South Tower of their church a bell whose sweet—if extremely frequent—ringing has been associated with Nantucket ever since. The Unitarians even today are so proud of the bell's clear tones that they ring it fifty-two strokes at sunrise, when sluggards are supposed to leap joyously from bed; fifty-two strokes at noon; and fifty-two strokes at 9 p.m. curfew—a total of 156 licks every single day. Some summer-visiting spoilsports, awakened at dawn after too gay an evening on the town, have asserted sourly that they would be just as happy if the bell were shipped back to Portugal, where it came from.

The bell was cast in Lisbon in 1810 for a Portuguese convent. But when the convent for some reason didn't take delivery, a Nantucket sea captain who couldn't resist a bargain bought it for $500. The Nantucket wags joked about the fact that a Catholic bell rang in a Unitarian Church for a Quaker town.

Prior to the War of 1812, most of the Nantucket houses were the conventional "lean-tos," similar to the Cape Cod "salt boxes." A typical lean-to is a snug, plain wooden house built around a central chimney, with two stories in the front and one story in the back. The Quakers believed that it was a sign of humility to live in a lean-to. When Job Macy built a house on Mill Street that had two stories on he back as well as the front, his father swore he'd never set foot in it—and he never did.

As the Quakers grew more and more prosperous, they started building little additions to their lean-tos. To show that they still had humility, though, the Quakers referred deprecatingly to their additions as "warts."

And then Joseph Starbuck, a rich ship-owner, defied tradition by building for his bride a house in New Dollar Lane which not only had two stories, front and back, but also two chimneys placed so that each of the eight rooms had its own fireplace. The whole town came to rubberneck while Joseph's house was being built, and the consensus was that he'd find out one of these days that Pride Goeth Before a Fall.

Three other rich men—Philip H. Folger, Frederick Mitchell, and Charles G. Coffin—soon rocked the town again by each building a brick house on Main Street. These three "bricks"—as the Quakers called them—quickly became the symbols of wealth and prosperity.

Joseph Starbuck gave the town still another rocking in 1837 when he announced that he intended to construct three more "bricks" on Main Street for his three sons, George, Matthew, and William. Old Joseph also shocked the Quakers by having Ionic pillars built at the doorways of the new "bricks." He himself drew the line at Corinthian columns, though. "Nothing with flowers," he told his architect firmly.

As though to fulfil the gloomy Quaker predictions about what would happen when Nantucketers lost their humility, a terrible fire swept through town July 13, 1846.

The blaze broke out in Will Geary's hat store, on the south side of Main Street. Ironically, lack of humility actually *did* play a part in the fire; because the blaze might have been extinguished quickly if two volunteer fire departments hadn't got into an argument about which would have the honor of playing its hose directly on the flames.

The fire burned for two days, and destroyed four wharves and about four hundred buildings, including practically every store and the Atheneum library. The damage wouldn't have been so bad if it hadn't been for amateur but well-meaning firefighters who blew up a number of houses in the path of the flames. Instead of stopping the blaze, these explosions only helped spread it.

Thanks to Mrs. Lydia Barrett, the "bricks" and a number of handsome wooden mansions on Main Street escaped with little or no damage. As the flames licked their way up toward Mrs. Barrett's house on Main Street near Fair, a group of frantic men raced into her living room bearing gunpowder kegs on their shoulders.

Mrs. Barrett calmly sat down on the top of the biggest keg, and announced:

"If thee are going to blow up my house, thee are going to have to blow up me with it."

The firemen argued and even tried to carry her forcibly out of her house. But while she played for time, the wind changed and they rushed away to do their damage elsewhere. If Mrs. Barrett's house had been blown up, the flaming debris almost certainly would have ignited the remaining residences in Main Street.

Incidentally, when the people whose houses *were* blown up tried to collect their fire insurance, a torrid legal battle developed. The insurance companies took the position that while they were obligated to pay fire losses, they couldn't be held responsible for stupid and premeditated explosions touched off by inane demolition crews. But as soon as the insurance companies expressed that viewpoint, Nantucketers countered swiftly by producing a whole parade of witnesses who testified that the roofs of the houses were blazing wildly, in every instance, before the gunpowder actually was touched off. And since it is well known that Quakers were always truthful, I guess that's the way it really was. At any rate, the companies had to pay for explosion damage as well as fire damage.

The town was quickly rebuilt, with local capital, money from the insurance claims, and $100,000 raised by public subscription "abroad," which is to say on the mainland. The new Atheneum library was a replica of the original.

But far more damaging to Nantucket than the fire were two other "catastrophes" for which there was no insurance: The building up of a sandbar at the entrance to the harbor and the discovery of kerosene.

There had been a sandbar at the harbor's mouth even before the first white settlers arrived, but it wasn't an obstacle to the little ships which first went whaling. As the bar started to grow higher, however, and as bigger ships replaced the smaller vessels, the obstruction threatened to put Nantucket out of business.

The ingenious Quakers didn't give up easily, though. Fifty of Nantucket's leading citizens contributed money to build a number of floating drydocks called "camels." The first of these devices, used to lift ships over the bar, was put in use in 1840. The camels worked satisfactorily, but they added so much to the cost of a voyage that more and more whaling ships started to use the port of New Bedford, instead of Nantucket. And to the Quakers' chagrin, New Bedford replaced the island as the whaling capital of the world.

But New Bedford's victory was short-lived, for whaling itself was doomed. While Nantucketers were rebuilding so hopefully after the Great Fire of 1846, simultaneous but independent experiments with new illuminating oils were being conducted in several small American shops and in one shop in Scotland. Incredible as it seemed to the Starbucks, the Coffins, and the Macys, two new types of "ile"—one made from coal and the other from petroleum discovered in Pennsylvania—were found to burn just as brightly as whale "ile."

The decline of whaling hit Nantucket so suddenly that thousands of people were thrown out of work. Business after business collapsed in panic. Because there was no employment for them at home, five hundred young men— a good portion of the island's life blood—went to California in the Gold Rush of 1849. The entire crew of the *Maria*, which happened to be in California at the time, gave up whaling and deserted to the diggin's.

The Quaker religion, divided by internal dissent dating back to the construction of the "bricks" and other mansions on Main Street, ceased to be an important influence. There was almost an hysterical note to the final jollification of the whaling days, when General Tom Thumb, the famous midget, visited Nantucket in 1850. The General drove through the streets in his miniature carriage, pulled by tiny ponies, and the ladies thought he

was so cute that they lined up to kiss him enthusiastically
—something that never would have been tolerated during
the Quakers' iron-handed rule.

The last whaleship sailed from Nantucket in 1869. The
population dropped from 10,000 in 1845 to 4,123 in 1870,
and 2,930 in 1905. The wharves rotted and grass grew between the cobblestones.

But don't feel too sorry for old Nantucket, because in
one way the island's loss proved to be a blessing. While
the rest of the country prospered and tore down its colo-
nial homes to make way for Victorian monstrosities, factories, hot dog stands, and filling stations, Nantucket was
too poor to engage in such "progress." So its cobblestoned
business section today remains much as it was back when
whale was king; its countryside is free of billboards; and
it has four hundred lean-tos, "bricks," and other dwellings
more than a century old.

Nantucket became solvent again when summer visitors
discovered that the island was "quaint." By that time, the
Nantucketers realized that they had a tourist asset in their
old homes and atmosphere, and that it was important to
keep everything just as it used to be.

So now the silver knockers and nameplates glisten again
on the doors of the Main Street mansions; the old lean-tos
have been re-shingled, spruced up and rented to tourists;
the wharfs have been rebuilt for yachts and small sailboats.

The proud old families take paying guests, but I don't
believe that Nantucket ever looked more prosperous than
it does today. And certainly it never looked so gay. I
should think that even a sour old Quaker would have

to admit that the climbing roses, hollyhocks, and cobalt-blue hydrangeas in almost every yard are an aesthetic improvement over spinach, turnips, and rape plants.

Nantucket today isn't a "reconstruction" of what it used to be, in the Williamsburg manner. It's the real thing—Nantucket architecturally is just as it always was.

Of course you won't find South Sea Islanders with filed teeth on the wharfs, but the "trippers" from Brooklyn and the Bronx—wearing the latest style of Bermuda shorts from Rowland Macy's store—are just about as interesting and colorful from a sociological standpoint.

Inside, the houses are mellowed, spick and span, and still as sound as the day they were built. The splendid, polished paneling glows like copper, and the exposed joists reveal the hand-hewn work of the ships' carpenters. Some of the big fireplaces are bricks made on the island, and held together with island clay.

Many of the houses are furnished with sperm-oil lamps, their wicks trimmed evenly; scrimshaw, rich mahogany furniture, wonderful old china. The front doors, for the most part, open onto the sidewalk, with no front yards. But the graceful back doorways lead to quiet little yards, bordered with white fences, boxwood and the flower gardens. The yards themselves usually have gates opening into narrow cobblestoned alleys.

As for the commons—or the "moors" as the summer visitors call them—they are a happy hunting grounds for artists and botanists. Mealy plum, heather, bayberries, Scotch broom, wild roses, huckleberries, Madonna lilies, and black-eyed Susans grow there. In the autumn, the huckleberry leaves turn a crimson orange, and from a distance the commons seem to be aflame. When the wild roses are blooming in July, you can smell them out at sea. In 'Sconset, the roses grow over the roofs of the little fishing shacks, with the "warts" attached, which have been made into summer cottages.

Oh, well. Let the Nantucket Chamber of Commerce do its own work!

15. SURREYS AND AUTOMOBILES

Summer visitors started coming to Nantucket in the 1840s, and in 1848 two summer hotels were built—the Ocean House in Nantucket and the Atlantic House in 'Sconset. When the last whaling ship returned to the island in 1870, Nantucketers made up their minds to go after tourists in a big way.

You couldn't expect people who had adventurously hunted whales around the world to sit back idly and wait for a tourist invasion. The islanders decided they'd develop Nantucket over night as a summer resort.

Real-estate booms were started at Surfside, Quaise, and Coatue. Madaket was subdivided into two thousand lots. Horsecars were installed. A railroad was built from Nantucket to 'Sconset via Surfside. The Riverside Hotel on the Providence River was dismantled and moved from Rhode Island to Surfside.

All of that seems incredible today, partly because the booms eventually burst and left little evidence of this enterprise, and partly because that sort of venturesome spirit simply doesn't exist any more on Nantucket. The hotel from Rhode Island collapsed in a heap in 1889 because of lack of repairs. The railroad and horsecars have long since disappeared. Coatue is uninhabited and Quaise is rolling moors. Madaket and Surfside are beginning to grow, but it's only been within the last thirty years that these two communities were "rediscovered" by the summer visitors.

Most of the land involved in the real-estate booms eventually was sold for non-payment of taxes, and many a Nantucket family lost whatever was left of its whaling fortune and—I'm afraid—whatever was left of its driving urge to make *another* fortune.

But just the same, visitors started to arrive in increasing numbers. As a young man in the 1870s and 1880s, my father spent some summers on Nantucket, and occasionally rode the train to 'Sconset, where he was courting a girl from New York. He used to swear that the train went so slow, as it tooted over the moors, that he could hop off, pick a bunch of Madonna lilies for his girl, and run along the tracks and catch it again.

President Grant was among the summer visitors in 1874. He stayed at the Ocean House, which is still in business today. Within the next ten or fifteen years, Presidents Arthur, Benjamin Harrison, and Cleveland came to the island to relax. Twice a day steamship service was in-

augurated in the summers, and a forerunner of the present
Chamber of Commerce advertised that on Nantucket
"summer is five Septembers long."

It took the Nantucketers some time to realize that the
summer visitors were attracted by the very thing that the
booms would have destroyed—a quiet atmosphere free
from crowds.

'Sconset's simplicity appealed to a number of prominent actors who Wanted to Get Away from It All. They
started a rustic summer colony, and within a few years
the former fishing village was the Newport of the theatrical world. Among those who stayed there were George
Fawcett, Digby Bell, DeWolf Hopper, Mary Mannering,
Daniel Frohman, and Lillian Russell. The informal per-
formances they gave at the 'Sconset Casino attracted
dramatic critics from New York and Boston, and the resulting publicity helped Nantucket's resort business.

By the time Dad brought us to Nantucket in 1918, the
theatrical capital was shifting from New York to Holly-
wood, and 'Sconset had more dilettantes than famous
actors. Also, the Nantucketers had definitely learned by
then that the best way to get summer visitors was to stop
the clock and specialize on "quaintness." Naturally, stopping the clock didn't have much appeal for young islanders, and more and more of them were migrating to the
mainland to get jobs.

The year-around population of the island in 1918 was
about twenty-eight hundred, and most of the people in
business seemed to be old men, universally addressed as
cap'n by the ten thousand or so summer visitors. The
cap'ns clerked in stores, took passengers sailing on fat

old catboats like the *Minnie R.*, and drove surreys-for-hire from the steamboat wharf to the hotels and from town to the bathing beach.

The old cap'ns, while living off the summer visitors, never were particularly fond of them. I suppose that the visitors, without realizing it, patronized the old men because they were poor and seemed provincial. I remember hearing one over-dressed woman on the steamboat wharf ask a white-bearded old-timer who was struggling to get her suitcase onto his surrey:

"Are you a native, Cap'n?"

To Nantucketers, "natives" are still South Sea Islanders. But the old man, who dated back to whaling days and had been to every corner of the earth, didn't want to get into an argument.

"Yep," he grunted. "Whoa, Freddie. Hold still, dammit."

"How wonderful. And have you driven one of those quaint carriages all your life?"

"Nope," he said. "I sta'ted out by pulling a Chinee rick-shaw right here on this same dock. It's only in the last two years, by collectin' fares from ladies like you, that I saved enough money to buy the hoss. Avast, gawddamya Freddie, or so help me I'll try you out for glue."

Even in 1918, Nantucketers were still undecided about the merit of automobiles. Some people thought that cars should be banned because they detracted from the island's "quaintness." Others said that if summer visitors couldn't bring their cars, they'd stop coming.

The first automobile had arrived on the island in 1900. It was a Stanley Steamer belonging to two Nantucketers, Arthur H. Folger and his son George. Nine years later,

Houghton Gibbs bought a discarded Fifth Avenue bus and put it into service between the town and 'Sconset. Clinton Folger brought an auto to the island in 1913, and used it on the mail run to 'Sconset. But the town banned cars in 1914, and thereafter Mr. Folger's machine was half wagon and half automobile. He had a team of horses pull his car from the Post Office to the town line, and then cranked up his engine and proceeded to 'Sconset. The vote banning cars was 376 to 234, and a Great Debate resulted which lasted four years and caused a good deal of hard feelings.

Another, and final, vote was held in May, 1918, and that time the pro-automobile faction won 336 to 296. A salesman for Maxwell cars arrived on the island on the next boat after the election, and two days later the whole town turned out to watch seven new cars drive off the steamer.

When we arrived on Nantucket in late June, automobiles were no longer a novelty. Dad himself didn't approve wholeheartedly of lifting the automobile ban, but he reasoned that since other people would have their cars there, he might as well have his. So he brought our gray Pierce Arrow touring car over from New Bedford on the Steamer *Gay Head*.

But if automobiles in general had ceased to be a novelty on Nantucket, *our* automobile—when filled with Dad, Mother and seven or eight children—still evoked more than passing comment.

Dad had been driving cars for years, but had a frightening accident record and never had mastered the technique of starting forward without a terrible lurch.

We'd try to brace ourselves and hold onto the babies,

when he'd grind the gears into low, toot his bulb horn, put out his hand, edge forward the throttle until the motor roared, and then ease his foot up off the clutch. But the series of tire-spinning, leaping lurches, which sometimes continued for half a block before the car made up its mind whether to proceed evenly or stall in protest, would shuffle our positions in the various seats, just the same.

Dad always blamed the clutch for these bucking starts, and in fact carried a face-saving can of Neatsfoot Oil in the tool kit, so that he could anoint the clutch after particularly embarrassing takeoffs which ended in stalls.

To drive with Dad through Nantucket's alley-sized streets was a spine-chilling, as well as a neck-cracking, experience. And it didn't add to our peace-of-mind to know that scores of Nantucketers, including some of the old surrey-driving cap'ns, were just learning how to operate cars.

There weren't any stop-streets in those days, but I doubt if Dad would have stopped anyway. He usually chose to ignore warning signs, on the grounds that compliance would only encourage the city fathers to new dictatorial extremes, such as cluttering up the beautiful landscape with even more signs. He also insisted that the Nantucket speed limit, plainly marked at twenty-five miles an hour, was probably meant to apply only to horses.

"They obviously just haven't got around to changing those signs yet," he'd tell Mother, when she nervously pointed out that he was going too fast.

Although the old cap'ns who were learning to drive were as much of a traffic hazard as Dad, the only accident that he had that summer involved the car of another summer resident.

Dad had driven all of us to 'Sconset, where a woman sold home-made ginger ice cream. On the return trip, he swung into Main Street by the old Rotch Market, narrowly missing the horse trough in the middle of the street, and jammed on his brakes to avoid hitting an empty Hupmobile, carelessly parked three or four feet from the curb.

Our car skidded to a halt about a foot from the rear of the Hupmobile, and stalled. I guess Dad had forgot to throw out the clutch. He tried the self-starter, but as usual it didn't function. Since there wasn't room between the two cars for Dad to get out and crank, he impatiently tooted our bulb horn for awhile, hoping that the driver of the other car would move his Hup.

When that didn't work, Dad climbed out of our car—no mean feat since there was no door on his side and he had to squeeze his rotund body past Mother and two babies on the front seat. Then he went to the Hup and angrily blew that horn.

The owner still didn't appear, but quite a crowd did. We were fairly used to that, so we ignored the onlookers, got out of the car, and helped Dad push our Pierce Arrow backward five or six feet. Then he cranked and cranked, always an exhausting and embittering experience, until finally the engine started. By the time he had crawled back behind the wheel again, he was wet with perspiration and in a black mood which the grinning spectators— making witticisms of the get-a-horse variety—did little to dispel. Of course he had to blame someone, so he kept muttering what he'd like to to the owner of the Hupmobile.

Dad backed the car away about twenty feet, in two leaping heaves. Then he ground the gears into low, speeded the engine, gave two toots on the bulb horn, and put out his hand. While we braced our feet on the floorboards and reached behind our necks to grab the top of the seat, he eased up on the clutch, and put the wheels to the left.

The car bounded forward, stopped on its haunches, shuddered, bounded forward again, stopped, leaped, and crashed into the rear of the Hup.

The onlookers burst into laughter, and although we still tried to ignore them, we were so embarrassed that two of the girls slipped down on the floor and hid under a steamer rug.

"That blasted clutch!" Dad said loudly, for the benefit of the onlookers. "Where's my Neatsfoot oil? I'd sure like to get my hands on the idiot who owns that Hupmobile."

Although the horn-blowing hadn't produced the Hupmobile owner, the sound of denting mudguards apparently had, because suddenly he was standing there at Dad's side of the car—and he was younger, taller, and more athletic looking than Dad. Indeed, almost *everyone* was more athletic looking than Dad, who weighed some two hundred and fifty pounds.

"Idiot, am I?" roared the Hupmobile owner. "Look what you've done to my car. I ought to punch you right in the nose."

During the many boxing lessons which Dad had enjoyed giving us, he had often recounted in some detail how, as a somewhat younger and slimmer man, he had dispatched such bullies with the aid of a fistic combination called the Magic Three—a left to the jaw, a right to the stomach, and a left uppercut again to the jaw. We waited tensely for the tanned and expensively dressed owner of the Hup to get his comeuppance.

"Let me see your license," was the best that Dad could come up with. To his credit though, his voice was steely and strong.

"*My* license? Why I wasn't any place near my car."

"Don't lose your temper, Dear," Mother urged Dad.

"Don't you worry about Daddy," I comforted her. "He'll show that big idiot the Magic Three, won't you Dad?"

"Right in the nose," sputtered the well-dressed summer visitor. "That's where I'd like to punch you."

"You'd better let Daddy out," one of my brothers told Mother. "He can't very well give the Magic Three when he's sitting behind a steering wheel, eh Daddy?"

"Hush," said Mother.

"What's the Magic Three?" asked the Hup owner, whose curiosity for a moment got the better of his temper.

"You'll find out soon enough, Mister," I promised him. "If there's going to be a nose-punching, Mister, you'll see who furnishes the nose, eh Daddy?"

"Hush," Mother insisted. "Let your father handle this."

"Right in the nose," said the Hup owner, returning to his original theme.

"You'd better let me out, Lillie," Dad sighed. "I think

I'm going to have to teach someone a lesson." He took off
his straw hat and his *pince nez,* and gave them to Mother
to hold. And you had to be proud of him. Soft, old, and
fat he might have been, but I don't believe he was afraid.
In fact, my brothers and I agreed later that there was a
trace of a hard smile at the corners of his mouth.

He squeezed over Mother and the two babies, and the
crowd edged in. But while Dad was getting out, the temper of the Hupmobile owner had a chance to cool. I guess
he didn't want a street brawl any more than Dad did, and
perhaps he had some sons of his own and began to realize
that Dad couldn't afford to lose face.

At any rate, he didn't mention nose-punching again.

"I don't think there's much harm done," he said. "Let's
see if we can't push them apart."

"All right," said Dad.

Some men in the crowd lent a hand, and in a few minutes the cars were separated. The damage was slight,
except for a broken headlight and a new dent in our front
fender, which bore the scars of many previous encounters.

"Do you have a self-starter?" the Hup owner asked Dad.

"Yes, but it doesn't always work."

"Same with mine. Why don't you get in and try it, and
if it doesn't work I'll spin the crank for you."

"Thanks," said Dad.

He started to climb over Mother and the two babies.

"You called his bluff, all right, eh Daddy?" said one of
my young brothers. "When the idiot saw you were going
to get out, he didn't want to fight any more, did he?"

"He shut up just like a clam," I agreed.

"Hush," warned Mother urgently. "That's enough now."

"I might be an idiot," grinned the Hup owner. "But I'm not idiot enough to want to go up against that Magic Three."

"Did you hear that, Daddy?" crowed my brother.

Dad retarded his spark and moved the ignition switch to "Battery." He advanced his throttle, gave three strokes to the gas priming pump, and tested the self-starter. For once it worked, and the engine roared to life. He waved to the Hup owner, put out his hand, blew the horn twice, shifted into low and eased up on the clutch. We braced ourselves, but for some reason the car glided smoothly away. Dad tooted the horn and waved again.

"That man sure turned yellow when Daddy got out of the car," my brother crowed again. "Did you hear what he said about being afraid of the Magic Three?"

Mother gave Dad back his glasses and his straw hat, and he put them on.

"Not so fast, John L. Sullivan," Mother smiled. "The signs say . . ."

Dad reached up and cocked his straw hat over his ear. Then he made a fist and held it under Mother's nose.

"Watch where you're going, John L.," giggled Mother.

"One more word about my driving and I'll give you the Magic Three," said Dad. "Those signs are for horses."

He edged the throttle forward and we pretty nearly hit the piazza of the Ocean House as we rounded a corner going like sixty, and took the road that leads up to The Cliff.

16. ADVENT OF THE TRIPPER

Nantucket today is as magically beautiful as ever. The old part of town still looks much as it did when Whale was King. There have been changes, of course, but some of them have been for the better. The wineglass elms still shade the blue-gray cobblestones of Main Street, and old men sit drowsily on benches under the trees. There's not a single billboard on the whole island. It's really a fact that summer *is* five Septembers long.

There are now about three thousand year-round residents and perhaps eighteen thousand summer residents and tourists who are known as "trippers."

Some of the twenty-room summer "cottages" which were built on The Cliff and near Brant Point in the days before the income tax, when people could afford to keep big staffs of servants, have been broken into smaller dwellings. One young man, an off-islander who has gone native, makes a living by dividing the old "cottages." He climbs up to the top of the roof with a handsaw and simply cuts a house into two, three, or four pieces. When he's finished sawing, he has a moving crew separate the pieces by a few feet. Then he uses one segment as a scaffolding to build a new side on another segment. Even some of the "warts" on the "cottages" built in the 1890s are big enough to make fair-sized summer homes today.

When I first came to Nantucket, it was an unwritten rule that the summer visitors did their swimming in the morning, and left the beaches to their servants in the afternoon. That's all changed now, and people feel free to go in the water whenever they choose. The Nantucketers are too busy in the summers to do much swimming, but they go to the beaches in late spring and early autumn.

The old-guard summer visitors now manage to struggle along with only one or two servants, and even no servants at all. The old-guarders belong to the Yacht Club, have a Beach Club of their own, and are unanimous in the belief that the trippers are ruining the island. The summer visitors look down their noses at the trippers, the trippers look down their noses at the Nantucketers, and the Nantucketers laugh up their sleeves impartially at both the summer visitors and the trippers.

Most of the trippers are young people from around New York, with a brief vacation and a limited budget. They descend on Nantucket from excursion planes and excursion boats, bearing vast impedimenta of spanking new athletic and sporting equipment—tennis rackets, golf clubs, fishing rods, surf boards, swimming goggles, fishing

spears, nets, creels, Scotch coolers, and so forth. A few of
them even carry riding crops and polo mallets. Their
pristine luggage often is encased in slip covers, so that it
won't get scratched or soiled. And their uniform is Bermuda shorts, rainbow-colored sport shirts, white athletic
socks, and sneakers.

They rent and ride English-type bicycles, fish off the
beach at unlikely places where no one has ever caught
anything but eel grass, and swim in front of the old public
bathhouse which the wealthy summer visitors patronized
before they retreated to the privacy of their relatively new
Beach Club.

The trippers started coming to Nantucket in large numbers right after World War II. At first, they shocked the
islanders and the summer visitors by wandering around
town in bathing suits. But the Board of Selectmen discour-
aged that by posting signs all over saying that such prac-
tices "simply weren't done."

Now most of the trippers change into bathing suits at
the public bathhouse. Others manage to change right on
the beach—although the town and the bathhouse operator
frown on that, too—underneath raincoats slipped over
their shoulders. A few walk or pedal to the beach with
bathing suits under their clothes, but this means a cold
and itchy trip back to town.

At the Beach Club, *everyone* changes in the bathhouse.
The old-guard summer residents wouldn't dream either of
coming to the beach in bathing suits or changing on the
beach. Since the bicycle is a trade-mark of the tripper, a
summer resident wouldn't get on one if you paid him,
and wouldn't get within ten feet of the tandem variety, on

which excited and intent tripper couples sometimes scorch along.

The trippers are noisy, but they are also quite gay—and it doesn't hurt to have some new young blood on the island. They *do* keep the Nantucket Cottage Hospital fairly busy, though, cutting fish hooks out of their backs and treating them for second-degree sunburn, charley horses and ankles sprained playing "tennis."

The trippers have been good for business, and a number of restaurants and stores have changed their names and their motifs to cater to them. During the 'Nineties, many of the restaurants stressed the whaling theme. Now—although I can't imagine why—some of the restaurants stress the theme of the 'Nineties, with cigar-store Indians and framed handbills of melodramas of the Lillian Russell period.

When I was a boy, it was required for gift and antique shops and restaurants in Nantucket and all along Cape Cod to feature what was supposed to be Old English spelling. That's passe now, and on Nantucket the Auld Curiosity Shoppe is gone and Lucky Pierre's does a thriving business.

As for the Nantucketers themselves, the tourist business of course is their bread and butter. They work hard in the summer, and take it fairly easy the rest of the year. A few make enough money to go to Florida, but most of them can't afford that, and in fact make barely enough to tide them over from one summer to the next.

The principal winter occupation is scalloping—and scallops weren't considered edible in the whaling days, or even much good for bait. It wasn't until 1880 that a market

developed for the "eyes," as Nantucketers called them
then. The first shipment of scallops from Nantucket occurred in January, 1881, and the money was a godsend.
Ever since then, scallops have been a limited but extremely welcome source of winter-time revenue.

The Nantucket women belong to sewing, quilting, book,
and bridge clubs, and visit around at each other's houses a
good deal in the winter. The men, besides scalloping,
spend the winter months building and repairing summer
homes, and swapping small talk. When there's nothing
better to do at night, some of them ride out to the town
dump, shine their headlights on the piles of refuse, and
shoot rats. As in the Quaker days, everyone knows exactly
what everyone else is doing. No secret sin, however minor,
remains a secret for very long.

The present day Nantucketer doesn't have the adventurous spirit of his great-grandfather. After all, if a man
were adventurous, why would he be living on Nantucket?
Certainly, the old whaling captains wouldn't have stayed
on present-day Nantucket for more than a week or two.
Look how they migrated to California in the Gold Rush,
when the whaling business began to slow down!

But the Nantucketer today is as independent as he ever
was. Nobody is going to tell him when to work, how to
work, or what to do. If you are nice to him and pay him
fairly, he may "help you out" by painting your window
frames or repairing your plumbing. But he comes to work
on his own terms and uses his own methods. If you don't
like the way he does a job, he shrugs and suggests that,
since you know so much about it, you do it yourself.

Some of the older Nantucket women, although quite

poor, would rather go hungry than sell land they have inherited. A couple of years ago, for instance, I tried to buy a small piece of a quite large vacant lot near our cottage and lighthouses. I went in to the Town Hall and found out that the land was owned by an old lady who lives in Orange Street.

"You think she'd sell me a piece of it?" I asked the clerk.

"Might," he conceded. "She could use the money, I know that."

So I drove up Orange Street, and knocked at the door of her snug, gray-shingled lean-to. She opened it, and she was quite old, but tall and straight, with heavy features and a purple shawl over her shoulders. I introduced myself, and she led me into a small sitting room, that I think must have been the old keepin' room. The coppery floorboards were eighteen inches wide, and the furniture probably had been made right there on Nantucket, two hundred years before.

"I remember you when your father used to ride all of you children around town in a big gray automobile," she smiled. "Gracious how time flies!"

We talked awhile, and then I asked her if she had ever thought of selling any part of her vacant lot.

"I've thought about it, yes," she nodded. "But I've decided against it."

"You wouldn't consider selling even a corner of it? I thought I'd like to build a cottage of my own there, near my family's place."

"I'd as soon sell it to you as anyone," she said, "but it's not for sale."

Then although I felt sure she wouldn't change her mind, I asked her anyway:

"Not at any price?"

"No."

"Do you mind telling me what you intend to do with the property?"

"Do with it!" she exclaimed, as if I had asked the most inane question in the world. "Do with it! Why *keep* it."

I remember once when I was a young boy, I got sleepy after Sunday supper at Nantucket. There is a sand dune, with a little pocket at the top, right in front of our house. The wind doesn't reach into the pocket, and when the sun's out the yellow sand is warm. I went out there and lay down on my back, watching the clouds change formation. It was still an hour or so before sunset. The air smelled clean and wonderful, as it always does on Nantucket. And how blue the sky was!

I could hear faintly the plop of conch shells being dropped by seagulls on the empty road to the Bathhouse, and then the squalls of protest as the gulls fought for the hermit crabs which scrambled for their lives from the shattered shells.

The baby was crying in our house, but I was used to that —so used to it that somehow it gave me a sense of security. I felt full of food, and warm, and good. Everyone I cared about in the world was right there in the cottage and the lighthouses. I thought that if somehow time should stand still, if the sun would never set, that I'd be content to lie there always watching the clouds, with nothing on my mind.

And the next thing I knew, my father was picking me up, and my mother was standing beside him. The sun had just gone down. Mother brushed some sand out of my hair, and Dad sat me down on his shoulders, as he had done back in the days when I was the "latest model."

"You know, Lillie," said Dad, reaching up to tickle the back of my neck, "I believe we'd better *keep* this one. Come on, boy. Bed's the place for you."

BIBLIOGRAPHY

Anatomy of Paradise, by J. C. Furnas. William Sloane Associates, New York, 1937.

An Island Patchwork, by Eleanor Early. Houghton Mifflin Company, Boston, 1941.

A Vanishing People of the South Seas, by John W. Church. *National Geographic Magazine,* October, 1919.

Bride in the Solomons, by Osa Johnson. Houghton Mifflin Company, Boston, 1944.

Brief Historical Data and Memories of My Boyhood Days in Nantucket, by Joseph E. C. Farnham. Joseph Farnham, Providence, 1923.

Cannibal Land, by Martin Johnson. Houghton Mifflin Company, Boston, 1921.

Captain Marooner, by Louis B. Davidson and Eddie Doherty. Thomas Y. Crowell Company, New York, 1952.

Dixie Raider, by Murray Morgan. E. P. Dutton and Company, New York, 1948.

From Off Island, by Dionis Coffin Riggs. Whittlesey House, New York, 1940.

History of Macy's of New York, by Ralph M. Tower. Harvard University Press, Cambridge, Massachusetts, 1946.

History of Nantucket, by Obed Macy. Macy and Pratt, Mansfield, Massachusetts, 1880.

History of Nantucket, by Alexander Starbuck. C. E. Goodspeed, Boston, 1924.

Letters from an American Farmer, by J. Hector St. John de Crèvecoeur. Thomas Davies, London, 1782.

Main Street, Nantucket, Massachusetts. Nantucket Historical Association, Nantucket, 1954.

Men and Manners in America One Hundred Years Ago, edited by H. E. Scudder. Scribner, Armstrong, New York, 1876.

Moby Dick, by Herman Melville.

Nantucket Argument Settlers, edited by Harry B. Turner. Inquirer and Mirror Press, Nantucket, 1936.

Nantucket Landfall, by Dorothy C. A. Blanchard. Dodd, Mead and Company, New York, 1956.

Nantucket Odyssey, by Emil F. Guba. Eaton Press, Watertown, Massachusetts, 1951.

Nantucket Scrap Basket, by William F. Macy. Houghton Mifflin Company, Boston, 1916.

Nantucket's Story, by Will Gardner. Whaling Museum Publications, Nantucket, 1949.

Nantucket, The Far-Away Island, by William Oliver Stevens. Dodd, Mead and Company, New York, 1936.

New Guinea Headhunt, by Caroline Mytinger. The Macmillan Company, New York, 1946.

Prominent Events from 1835–1880, by William C. Macy. Macy and Pratt, Mansfield, Massachusetts, 1880.

Pursuing the Whale, by John A. Cook. Houghton Mifflin Company, Boston, 1926.

Quakerism on Nantucket, by Burnham N. Dell. Nantucket Historical Association, Nantucket, 1955.

Rambling Through the Streets and Lanes of Nantucket, by Edouard A. Stackpole. Inquirer and Mirror Press, Nantucket, 1947.

Sweeper in the Sky, by Helen Wright. The Macmillan Company, New York, 1950.

The Clock That Talks, by Will Gardner. Whaling Museum Publications, Nantucket, 1954.

The Great Merchants, by Tom Mahoney. Harper and Brothers, New York, 1955.

The Great Story of Whales, by Georges Blond. Hanover House, Garden City, New York, 1955.

The Last King of Paradise, by Eugene Burns. Farrar, Straus, & Cudahy, Inc., New York, 1952.

The Loss of the Essex. Inquirer and Mirror Press, Nantucket, 1935.

The Real Story of the Whaler, by A. Hyatt Verrill. Appleton-Century-Crofts Co., Inc., New York, 1916.

The Story of Old Nantucket, by William F. Macy. Houghton Mifflin Company, Boston, 1915.

The Voyage of the Huron and the Huntress, by Edouard A. Stackpole. Connecticut Printers, Hartford, 1955.

Three Bricks and Three Brothers, by Will Gardner. Houghton Mifflin Company, Boston, 1945.

When New England Saw the Serpent, by Evarts Erickson. American Heritage, New York, April 1956.

Wrecked on the Feejees, compiled from the log-book of

William S. Cary by Harry B. Turner. Inquirer and Mirror Press, Nantucket, 1928.

Yankee Whalers in the South Seas, by A. B. C. Whipple. Doubleday & Company, Garden City, New York, 1954.